I Love to Go a Wandering

Magical Memories of Molineux Wolves

By
Lawrence Kilkenny

Copyright © 2017 Lawrence Kilkenny

Table of Contents

INTRODUCTION 1

Chapter 1: Ah Day Say That!.. 9

Chapter 2: 1954 and All That...................................... 19

Chapter 3: Three Magical Seasons............................. 29

Chapter 4: 1957-60 continued.................................... 37

Chapter 5: Running Away from It All 49

Chapter 6: Four in a Row... 63

Chapter 7: Nothing for 57 Years................................. 69

Chapter 8: Freezing, Baking and Soaking................. 77

Chapter 9: Peter and Norman.................................... 85

Chapter 10: Away from Home.................................... 91

Chapter 11: Wembley and Cardiff 99

Chapter 12: Glory Hunters..105

Chapter 13: Them Lot down the Road....................111

Chapter 14: Let's Have a Sing-Song.........................117

Chapter 15: Need'st Thou Run So Many Miles About? (William Shakespeare's Richard III)............125

Chapter 16: Some Matches You Never Forget.......131

Chapter 17: That Atmospheric Night 137

Chapter 18: My Family and Lots of Animals 143

Chapter 19: Lost in the Mists of Time 149

Chapter 20: Attendance Record..157

Chapter 21: Season Ticket Holder 165

Chapter 22: Some of My Favourite Players....................171

Chapter 23: Parkinson's Awareness...................................181

Chapter 24: Keeping Fit..193

Chapter 25: More of My Favourite Players....................197

Chapter 26: The Good Times and the Bad......................207

Chapter 27: What a Club Is Wolves!...................................215

Chapter 28: I Hate... 225

Chapter 29: There's Only One Wanderers 231

Chapter 30: Tying up Loose Ends 237

Chapter 31: Au Revoir, Not Goodbye.................................245

EPILOGUE...253

ACKNOWLEDGEMENTS

There are many people I would like to thank for their contributions in helping me to write this book and who have in other ways been extraordinarily kind to me when they learned of my Parkinson's condition.

Firstly, without my Wolves "bible", namely the superb *The Wolves (An Encyclopaedia of Wolverhampton Wanderers Football Club 1877 - 1989)* by Tony Matthews (with Les Smith) I would have been floundering to remember statistical information, such as dates of matches, goal scorers and size of attendances. I am greatly indebted to their monumental efforts in producing this tremendous tome, a must-have reference book for any Wolves fan.

No book is complete without its cover and what a cover TrueWolf has designed for me out of the kindness of his heart. TrueWolf is his chosen name on the Molineux Mix internet forum, so a thousand thanks, my friend, for designing the cover so professionally, and exactly to my liking and desire.

TrueWolf offered his professional services free and gratis when he and the club heard that I was ceasing attendance at football matches at Molineux after 60 years, because of advancing Parkinson's Disease. Other Molineux Mixers, including arctic rime and PumpKing, and Wolves' Marketing Manager, Laura Gabbidon, plotted a send-off that I will never forget - a private box from which to watch the final match of the 2016-17 season with my friends. I cannot thank them enough.

I also wish to thank Wolves' Vice-President and scoring legend, Steve Bull, and current marauding wingback, Matt Doherty, for taking the time to make my final day at Molineux so special.

And finally, many thanks to the family of Wolves supporters, especially the Molineux Mixers, and all my friends in the Steve Bull Stand and in my village, who have shown such kindness to me in so many ways. I hope you enjoy this book, which is dedicated to you all.

INTRODUCTION

Perhaps the title of this book led you to believe it was a story about someone getting back to nature and living a life with a strange breed of lupine beasts? If that is so, you will be disappointed and had better put the book back on the shelf; if, however, you like stories of infatuation and love and romance (with a lot of football, running and animals thrown in), then keep the book in your basket and enjoy reading it when you get home. This is a story of love and infatuation but it isn't a tale of love between two people; rather, it is about a passionate association between a person and a sporting organisation.

It is about my almost life-long love affair with a football team. It is typical, perhaps, of the story of any fan's affection for his or her club, but this isn't about just any football team - it's about Wolverhampton Wanderers, the Wolves, my team, resident in the beautiful stadium with the evocative name of Molineux. In its prime, this stadium contained the biggest Kop in the land, accommodating 30,000 fans, the greatest team in the world situated proudly in a good, honest, working-class town in the Black Country. There is only one football team associated with the name of Wolves, and it is my team and my love.

The main title of this book contains the opening words to the tune that was played, back in the 1950s, when

Wolves ran out onto the pitch just prior to the start of a match. We all love to go a wandering, in support of our beloved team.

This book is also about a strange and devilish fellow, Mr P. He is no other than the evil personification of Parkinson's Disease (PD); for this is a story, too, about how I have suffered from the cursed and challenging condition in my later years, and the battles I waged as I tried to dislodge the parasitic Mr P from my shoulder. Eventually, however, Mr P prevailed and forced me into ceasing my trips to my beloved Molineux Stadium. But it is, at the same time, a story of hope and optimism, both for the Wolves and for Parkinson's sufferers, including myself.

I am setting down these memories in the summer of 2017. In November of this year I will be celebrating the diamond jubilee of my first visit to Molineux, on 2nd November 1957, when I saw Wolves play Nottingham Forest and emerge victorious by two goals to nil. The last match of this current season, 2016-17, versus Preston North End, will probably be my last visit to the hallowed ground. Parkinson's Disease now has me in its grip and that grip is ever-tightening. I think the time has come to retire from football attendance gracefully, just as Billy Wright and Bill Slater and Steve Bull and Malcolm Finlayson, and many others, have done before me, hanging up their boots when they knew that the time to call it a day had arrived for them.

I want to get these reminiscences recorded before Mr P has a go at my mind. He and I have been fighting over my body for a good number of years now but, so far, my mind has been a no-go area for him. Let's keep it that way! However, as all 75-year olds will know, memory isn't what it was when we were younger, and some memories of past events and of matches attended long ago are vague and cloudy, if not obliterated entirely in the mists of time. However, other memories are still alive and bright, clear and vivid and capable of being recalled, and these are the memories I want to tell you about in the pages of this book.

And so, I can clearly remember and picture the two goals Wolves scored in the first away match I ever attended, at Burnley in 1958; I can hear, as if it were yesterday, the stamping feet on the North Bank floorboards on a bitterly cold day in 1963 and I can still recall the ecstatic emotions generated by the 6-0 half-time lead and the second-half blizzard in the Portsmouth match of 1965. I can remember the humour of the Den Haag UEFA Cup match, but I have no recollection of the goals in the last match of 1957-58 when we sealed the Championship with a 2-0 win against Preston, even though I was a spectator at the match and was amongst those dancing on the pitch afterwards, a member of the jubilant crowd. Some memories are undiminished by the passage of time while others have faded into oblivion.

I am greatly indebted, as I stated on the Acknowledgements page, to the wonderful encyclopaedia *The Wolves* by Tony Matthews (with Les Smith), *An Encyclopaedia of Wolverhampton Wanderers Football Club 1877 - 1989,* which has been my bible in researching this book, and has enabled me to look up facts I had long forgotten, such as precise dates of matches, the names of scorers and the size of the crowds, if I could not recall these statistics for myself. But if I have no memories of a certain match or incident, I will say so and not pretend that I do recollect it.

I will tell you about the glory days of the late 1950s, when I first went to Molineux, and about the wonderful players who graced our great team then and trod the hallowed Molineux turf. And I will recount other incidents of interest and humour down the years, up to the present day. I will describe how my running career interacted and, at times, clashed with my football support, without trying to justify my relative love for either one of them.

I hope you will find this account interesting and entertaining. It is not a history of Wolverhampton Wanderers but a personal account of my 60 years association with the Wolves. It is by no means comprehensive, nor is it in chronological order, and it is not meant to be. These are the random musings of this and that, mostly covering the contrasting decades of the fifties and the sixties, by a mature (not to say ancient) Wolves supporter, who was not particularly loyal in his regular match attendance over the years, but who held allegiance to no other club but Wolves. It contains my opinions and my judgements, which may not necessarily agree with yours. But, then, you can always counter my prejudices by writing your own book, containing your own memories and opinions.

I hope I haven't been disrespectful to any other clubs or their supporters in these pages. I have poked gentle fun at certain teams from time to time but I have never despised any side or its fans. All football followers are fans of the beautiful game and, maybe, supporters from clubs other than Wolves will find this book an interesting read too. We all come in peace, possessed by the same infatuation - our love of football.

Perhaps what I am trying to say is summed up in the love poem on the next page, which I posted on the Molineux Mix internet forum in 2017 as my farewell to Molineux. It's not the only piece of verse you will find in this book, but perhaps it is the best, coming, as it does, directly from the heart.

The older fans of Wolverhampton dream
Of glory days which happened long ago;
O happy times, when their beloved team
did almost win three titles in a row.
The fifties' Wolves were virtually supreme;
They were respected by both fan and foe.
These days I'm full of aches and pains and cramps;
But then I partied - Wolves were English champs!

I first stood on the Kop in '57;
In those days, you could move around quite freely.
A young lad, I was lifted up to Heaven
by goals from Broadbent and from Norman Deeley.
It was a quite stupendous first eleven,
The forwards full of goals, the rear-guard steely.
The Wolves defence was almost water-tight,
With Harris, Clamp, Stuart, Flowers and Billy Wright

This year will be my diamond anniversary
of that first schoolboy trip to Molineux.
Although then only twelve years out of nursery
Already I adhered to Wolves like glue.
They were the top team - just no controversy;
the team with kit of black and golden hue.
I'll follow them from now until my death
And cheer them with my final, dying breath

Chapter 1
Ah Day Say That!

You claim I said his nickname's "mAnkey".
Ah day, ah told you it was "mOOnkey".
Your hearing's faulty, it appears,
So, hurry home and wash your ears.

Now, just because I'm from the south,
Don't mock what issues from my mouth.
My accent isn't who I am;
A Southerner or plain Yam-Yam.

> *Now how I speak or how I talk,*
> *Or how I use my knife and fork*
> *Do not define me - no, by gosh.*
> *I may be plain, I may be posh.*
>
> *It's how I live and work and play,*
> *(not how I speak the words I say),*
> *That both determine who is me*
> *And show my personality.*

I didn't support the Wolves, or any other football team for that matter, in my younger years; in fact, I wasn't into professional football at all and had no knowledge or interest in it. The only recollection of anything football-related which I can recall from my early childhood was being belted in the face from point-blank range by a heavy leather football, dispatched at high speed by my games teacher, from a few feet away - not deliberately, I hasten to add. I went home with a very red face that day, which alarmed my mother considerably.

The rest of this chapter describes my upbringing and the circumstances in which I came to know and love the Wolves.

I was born towards the end of 1941, a war baby, arriving the year after the Battle of Britain, and I can still recall the hideous whine of the air raid sirens, warning of likely attack, and the relief of hearing the All Clear signal. It was very frightening for a young boy, not yet four years old by the time of VE Day.

I was brought up in the harshness and deprivation of the 1940s and the early 1950s when rationing was endemic and food and luxuries sparse, and appreciated all-the-more when they were available. My dad had fought in and survived the horrors of the trenches in the so-called Great War and was in the Home Guard (or Dad's Army) in Hitler's war. My mum reared a family of six - I was number three in the brood - and she never worked again after she married my dad in 1931 (that's if you call bringing up six children in times of hardship and rationing 'not working'). Football was no part of my being or consciousness in those early years of my life, and I'd never even heard of Wolverhampton Wanderers.

In fact, I was quite a sickly child. My mum was unable to provide me naturally with the nutrients I required because she herself was malnourished by the deprivations of rationing and from the comparative poverty under which our family existed. And, consequently, I developed the bone disease, rickets. The remedy was to put me out in the sunshine in my pram, wearing little or nothing, to soak up the vitamin D my bones required. I am sure this sunbathing wasn't imposed on me until my first winter was over and the warm spring sunshine had made an appearance - I don't think I was expected to sunbathe on frosty days! I grew up a weak and ailing child and was anything but sporty or at all interested in following sport. Wolves were unheard of and not part of my life. Wolverhampton - what or where was that?

Two sisters put in their appearances in 1943 and 1945 as additional siblings to me and my older brother and sister, and my baby brother was born in 1949, to become, like me, a future Wolves supporter. He arrived in August of that year, when I was not yet eight years old, and such was my ignorance of, or indeed, interest in, football that I was totally unaware that Stan Cullis, the Wolves manager, and Billy Wright, the skipper, had both celebrated their first trophy successes three months earlier, as Wolves won the FA Cup for the third time in their history. And why should we have known or cared about an event which was, for us, such an obscure item of news? We were living in the green and pretty counties of Oxfordshire and, later, Berkshire and hadn't even heard of Staffordshire, where Wolverhampton was then located, or even of the Midlands. The future six-decades-long love affair with a group of men kicking a ball around the football pitches of

England and the world was not yet a twinkle even in the Almighty's eye.

My health didn't allow me to start school until I was six years old, and I remember having much time off, once I did start, for one ailment or another. I remember the huge snow falls of 1947, the snow rising level with the tops of the hedges, and I remember also that we were marooned in the house for several days - and then came the thaw and floods; rivers of water gushed down the roads in torrents outside our house.

When I was five I contracted whooping cough, as did my younger sisters, aged three and two at the time. I remember the big pram which my mum wheeled to the shops with baby sister inside, second sister sitting on the front frame and yours truly clutching his mum's hand and legging it, the three of us young ones whooping loudly down the street. You wouldn't get a pram that big on the back seat of a family car today - but, then, very few people had cars in those times. My mum used to walk the mile to the shops most days to buy fresh food. There were no fridges or freezers around then - and certainly not in our house.

My mum told me I refused to acknowledge that I had the whoops and would hide under the blankets at night to whoop away in privacy without being heard. Apparently, the remedy for the complaint was to take to the skies in a plane, a course of action unfortunately not available to us (it would have been fun, we thought). Eventually, the whoops went away, as they inevitably do in the end.

I had great fun growing up and playing with my sisters in the countryside, big brother being almost seven years older and off doing his own thing. I learned how to cycle by purloining my big sister's bike; it was much too large for me and I couldn't locate the brake lever, so the only way to stop the machine was to direct it into the neighbour's garden wall, with a hefty thump. The bike and I survived the impact (and so did the garden wall - fortunately for me, I've no doubt!).

When we were all old enough to own our own bikes, I went out for a spin with my three sisters, the four of us riding abreast and linking hands, the two outer riders handling the steering (I use the term "handling" quite loosely). Of course, we collapsed in a tangled heap of bike frames, pedals, handlebars, oily chains and bodies, my big sister on the bottom and yours truly nestling securely and protectively on the top of the pile. Our fall was cushioned by landing on a soft bed of stinging nettles, so happily there were no bruises or broken bones. I don't know if my sister thought this was an entirely successful ending to the bike ride or not - but are you beginning to wonder how this future Wolves supporter survived to ever make it into Molineux?

My mother was the best mum it was possible to have. She lived a life of devotion to her family and was always available to provide for our every need and to give solace in times of difficulty and trial. She contracted Parkinson's in her later years and bore it so bravely. The night she died in hospital she called out for the duty nurse to attend to a lady in the next bed who was shouting out for help. My mum was thinking of other people rather than herself right up to her last breath. She was, and is, my pride and inspiration as I now battle the wretched condition myself.

School was one mile away and we walked there each morning, retraced our steps home for lunch, returned to school in the afternoon and finally walked back home again for tea. Those four miles of walking each day laid the basis, I am convinced, for my fitness and my later athletics career. My mum's school run consisted of walking us there in the morning and meeting us for the home walk at the end of the day, so she did four miles too. My rickets had now been conquered and I was growing up to be a reasonably fit and healthy boy.

My dad was employed as a civilian clerk in the Air Ministry, which entailed frequent postings to different RAF stations. In our Berkshire days, he worked at the RAF bases of Abingdon, Culham and Didcot and was later promoted to the considerably responsible position of Civilian Welfare Officer. He generally travelled to work by bicycle, on a ponderous and heavy machine with a non-adjustable gear (I think he might have reached 10 miles per hour with a favourable wind at his back). And then, in 1953, fate saw him posted to RAF Cosford in Shropshire and we were about to uproot ourselves from the leafy lanes of Berkshire to the cold, northern wastes of the Midlands. Wolverhampton, here we come!

My dad blazed a trail ahead of us and, for a few months, house-hunted in the Cosford area while the rest of the family waited behind in Abingdon. For as long as I can remember Dad had "invested" in the football pools, and the five minutes from five o'clock to five minutes past five on a Saturday night were sacrosanct, as he checked his coupon against the radio (we called it 'the wireless' in those days) announcer's words on "Sports Report", read by Eamon Andrews or Raymond Glendenning in the early days, if I recollect correctly. "SHHHHH!" was hissed at anyone misguided enough to utter a sound during those hallowed five minutes. Inevitably, the results were disappointing, causing him to rip up the coupon and turn off the wireless after the five minutes were up. Perhaps if he had left the wireless on I might have learned a bit about Wolves, and football in general, and so prepared myself better for later years.

While he was living away from us we still tuned into the wireless (I think it was the Light Programme, but it might have been the Home Service) to listen to the results, just for something to occupy us, really, and to maintain a link with Dad. Knowing that Wolverhampton was in the area where he was house-hunting, we listened for that one out of curiosity: "Middlesbrough 3 Wolverhampton Wanderers 3". My four-year-old brother intoned "Wulderhanton Wanderers", and so was born our first, tenuous connection with the sacred name.

In November 1953, a house having been found at last, we all piled onto a train at Oxford station and travelled via Banbury and Leamington Spa to, what seemed to us, the grim Dickensian landscape of the Birmingham industrial conurbation. Even grimmer to us was the vista of industrial dereliction which assailed our eyes on the second train, from Brum to Wolverhampton, but we were back in our accustomed rural setting as the third and final train carried us via Codsall to Albrighton, the village where we were to live for the next five years or so. Our new home was very close to RAF Cosford; in fact, just a farmer's field intervened between our garden and the airfield take-off strip (we received a severe dressing down from the farmer when he caught us playing on his property - "you didn't ought to be in this field").

Albrighton was just within the county boundary of Shropshire, although bearing a Staffordshire postal address, and my dad, a devout Catholic and a man of deep principle, was having a battle with the local authorities to get me into the nearest catholic grammar school, over the border in Staffordshire. They wanted to send me to Wellington in Shropshire but he was adamant it should be the nearer school in Wolverhampton. He finally won the day and I was soon to become a pupil of St Chad's Grammar School for Boys in Oldfallings Lane, Wolverhampton. The dispute with the two councils, however, delayed my start and I didn't begin until January 1954. In the meantime, we purchased my school uniform from the school's suppliers, Green and Hollins, enjoyed window shopping in Beatties' department store and partook of refreshments in Lyons Corner Shop in Queen Square.

And so, when the day came to start the new term at St Chad's there was I, naked and exposed, the new boy on the block, with the gawky appearance and the funny posh southern accent, fair game for fun and ridicule by the ruthless locals.

"It's 'muunkey', not 'mankey'" they would scold me. However, although I knew I didn't pronounce the word like they did, I nevertheless couldn't detect any similarity between how I pronounced it (with my soft 'uh' sounding vowel) and the short 'a' sound of the cockney, which they claimed was how they thought I did, in fact, pronounce the word. But they wouldn't have it and so I conceded: "OK, then, it's 'mooonkey', if you insist".

Someone standing out from the norm will always be a target for attention and ridicule but I was fortunate that, a few weeks on from when I started at the school, a boy even posher than me joined us and the Midlanders turned their merciless attentions to him, leaving me comparatively free to marvel at their accents and to try to acquire the same for myself, so that I could stay out of further trouble. To this day I have a passably good Midlands (I wouldn't say Wolverhampton) accent which lapses back into Berkshire when I am with my siblings.

Talking of accents, there's a big man who sits two seats from me in the Steve Bull stand. He is the nicest and kindest person you could wish to meet but so large you wouldn't want to encounter him down a gloomy alley on a dark night. He speaks very rapidly and, I'm afraid, in such a broad accent that I can't understand a word he says. Come to that, nor can most other people who sit round about us. We think he might come from Gornal or Dudley or, possibly, Walsall; but he wears his heart very much on his sleeve and I have seen the tears roll down his cheeks at promotion moments and seen him storm out in disgust on other occasions, 10 minutes before the end of the match, when things haven't been going so well.

And so, I started off on the wrong foot with my career at St Chad's, not so much by what I said as by how I said it. However, there was a far, far worse crime than my non-Wolverhampton accent, which I was guilty of, although I didn't realise it at the time. Innocently enough I turned up at school on my first morning, sporting a nice new scarf - a blue scarf, fetchingly adorned with white stripes! I thought it contrasted nicely with the orangey scarves of my contemporaries. They probably thought it contrasted with their scarves too, but not very nicely.

Chapter 2
1954 and All That

Why have you colours blue and white - all round your face?
You know you should have gold and black - you're a disgrace!
Go, tell your mum you've changed the spec
For what you'll wear around your neck.

The scarf you wear to school is all - stripy and saggy,
But it would not look out of place - on any Baggie.
As language classes teach the present tense,
NOW get a gold scarf - it makes perfect sense.

I didn't start going to football matches until I was in Form 5 (Year 11), being more concerned with studies, and singing in the girls' chorus in the Gilbert & Sullivan operettas, staged by the school each summer in the Wulfrun Hall. How did I come to be performing opera in drag? Well, most of the new intake of boys into Form 1 each year possessed high-register, boy-treble voices, and our music teacher, a fanatical G & S devotee, auditioned every boy (I think it was compulsory to take part) to see if his voice could hold a note, or whether the owner of the voice was tone-deaf. The assembled boy-treble chorus performed so well that captivated members of the audience remarked to the gratified music teacher: "That was wonderful. I never realised St Chad's was a mixed-gender school!"

I sang in "The Mikado" and in "Ruddigore", but then my voice broke and it was not up to much after that, so the opera producer cast me aside onto the operatic scrapheap! Because of all this activity I completely missed out on the historic events of the 1953/54 football season.

The first part of 1954 was the most momentous time in Wolves history, the year they won the English Championship for the first time in their, then, 77 years history. And what a battle it was with their nearest (and dearest?) neighbours and arch rivals, West Bromwich Albion. The two teams went head to head and toe to toe throughout the season and in the end Wolves pipped Albion to the title by 57 points to 53, a margin of two wins (it was just two points for a win in those days).

Absolutely crucial to Wolves' ultimate success were two 1-0 victories against the local enemy, one in November, when Jimmy Mullen scored at the Hawthorns, and the other in April, when Roy Swinbourne notched the winner at Molineux. 56,590 and 49,884 watched the respective matches. Had the games ended in West Bromwich Albion's favour they would have taken the title by the same 57 to 53 points' margin. Despite missing out on the league title West Brom enjoyed the rich consolation of lifting the FA Cup at the end of the season, our showing in the competition that year being best forgotten - we lost 1-2 at home to 2nd division Birmingham City in the third round! So not only the Midlands but the Black Country itself made a clean sweep of the two major trophies competed for at that time. Such a local dominance has never occurred again since then.

And while all this was going on I was turning up at school wearing a blue and white striped scarf!

My awareness of football, local or otherwise, was still virtually non-existent. I was a bit of a loner and tended to come in on the bus, do lessons and then return to my rural idyll. I was painfully shy at that time and made few friends.

I was a bit of a swotty type and English was my strong subject, but I was very poor at sport. There was no chance of getting into the school football teams, which were very strong and competed in the local inter-schools' league. However, I was drafted in to the House team for Wednesday afternoon matches, mainly because of a lack of available players to make up the numbers, and I usually played left half where, it was felt, I could cause the least harm.

On one memorable occasion I strolled forward, bored with the play, which was predominantly taking place on the right wing, on the far side of the pitch, and leaving me isolated on the left. Suddenly the ball drifted across the empty penalty area from the right-hand side, the goalie was nowhere to be seen (nor was anybody else except me) and all I had to do was tap the said ball over the line for a goal - I was even able to stay onside. I was quite pleased with myself but, when I told my House Master that I had scored, he was less than impressed: "What were you doing up that end of the field? You're supposed to stay back to support your defence. You don't go wandering off and deserting your post like that."

Well, thanks for that! He obviously hadn't seen Ron Flowers play in the left half position for Wolves (neither had I, for that matter). Incidentally, this was the same man who nurtured my love of English and I am forever grateful to him for his scholarly tuition, notwithstanding his curmudgeonly reaction to my goal.

As an aside, I am using obsolete terms here for positions on the football pitch. Teams played a 2-3-5 formation with two full backs (right and left), three half backs (right, centre and left) and five forwards (outside and inside left and right, and centre forward). As that was how we referred to positions back in the 50s I will continue to use this nomenclature whilst writing about those times; but back to the scarf.

I was challenged about it a few times on the trolley bus into town.

"Who are you supporting then?"

"What? Erm - I don't know. I haven't decided yet." I had no idea what they were talking about.

"You haven't decided yet! You'd better be quick about it. It'll all be over, come May."

I thought they must have been referring to a House competition, or something like that. I daresay the school harboured some Baggies' supporters but, if so, they kept their heads down and none of them was brave enough to own up to their allegiance. They might have even worn gold scarves to disguise their leanings, as I saw no scarf-less boys during the winter months, and certainly none wearing blue and white stripes! Only I, the shy newbie, seemed prepared to come out, apparently wearing my club colours with pride, only to deny allegiance when confronted.

Slowly it dawned on me that exciting things were happening in the town of Wolverhampton and I began to take an interest in the results, and was pleased when Wolves won. The floodlit friendlies against Spartak and Honved were thrilling to read about in the papers but we didn't have a telly on which to see the spectacle in all its glory. My wife's uncle, now 90 and an ardent Liverpool supporter all his life, tells me of the nights in 1954 when most of his brothers (of which he had five) crowded round the TV set in Liverpool in the house of the only one of the six of them rich enough to possess one. They watched the match, which was displayed in black and white on the tiny screen, enthralled by the thrilling exploits of Wolves against Honved and Spartak. Not only Wolverhampton was gripped by Wolves' displays - the whole nation was enthused by them as well.

And to add the icing to the cake, we won the Championship for the first time, though this fact obviously passed me by.

The next three seasons drifted by and Manchester United's Busby Babes took over the mantle of champions, after Chelsea had just pipped us to a second successive title in 1954-55. At the start of the 1957-58 season football fervour at last began to grip me properly. Wolves beat the defending champions, Manchester United, a chap called Deeley was reported to be scoring lots of goals and it seemed like a good idea to go along and see what it was all about.

At our school, we played House football or cricket matches on Wednesday afternoons and then caught up on academic work on Saturday mornings. This made it hard for me to attend matches, had I wished to do so, since I would have had to travel back home for lunch and then back over to Wolverhampton to see the match. Pocket money wouldn't stretch to a double journey - I think I was getting two shillings and sixpence (twelve and a half pence) by then and it might have been one shilling and sixpence to get into the ground as a schoolboy. The bus fare to town, I remember well, was four pence halfpenny for a schoolboy.

My finances would have been stretched to the limit, but then the obvious answer presented itself - why not stay over to see the match and then go home? And so, on 2nd November 1957, I did just that.

I felt almost unworthy as I stepped into, what seemed, the Holy of Holies as I clicked my way through the turnstiles into Molineux on my own for the very first time, almost in trepidation at having the gall to enter the great shrine of football. I came into the famous stadium at the top of the South Bank and gasped at the view from the highest Kop in the country. I settled at a crush barrier about halfway down, just under the roof, read the programme and soaked up the atmosphere, still having an hour to wait until kick-off. It was well worth the wait.

What a privilege it was to see Billy Wright running out, carrying the ball and leading his team. I don't remember whether they came out first or whether it was Nottingham Forest but, after a short kick around, the match was underway; no extensive warm-up drills, reception line-ups or huddles in those days. Incidentally, I hate today's receptions, where one team stands in a line and the other saunters down that line, perfunctorily shaking hands with their opponents, with absolutely no eye contact taking place - at least, that's how it appears to me on the TV. Either greet your opponents in a friendly fashion or skip that bit of meaningless ritual.

I recall little of that first match, 59 years and five months ago as I write, and it's only by reference to the archives that I know that Peter Broadbent and Norman Deeley scored and we won the match two-nil. It was little Norman Deeley's 13th goal of the season, all scored from the wing, and achieved from the 14 games in which he had featured out of the 15 that had been played. He became my second most favourite player and I loved to see him jinking down the wing with his arms down by his sides and palms turned downwards and outwards as if he was attempting a pirouette, with the ball at his feet. Who was my most favourite player? In case you hadn't guessed, it was Norman's mate, Peter Broadbent!

It was magical just being there, although the players looked as small as Subbuteo men, way down below, and I understood little of what was going on. But I was watching the team, that I already loved, for the very first time, amongst a crowd of nearly 48 thousand kindred souls, and that occasion can never be taken away from me. It was love at first sight, and that love continues unabated to this day.

I saw Wolves (now my team, to the exclusion of all others) take on West Bromwich Albion in the next home match a fortnight later. This time, I took my two younger sisters with me - they had been clamouring to attend after hearing all about the Forest match, and seeing Wolves topping the table (I think they must have been glory hunters!) We were in the North Bank and my youngest sister being only 12 and quite small, we sat on the wall at the front for a pitch-level view of the game. Consequently, we hadn't much idea of what was happening at the South Bank end of the ground. The match ended in a one-one draw with Eddie Clamp scoring from a penalty kick at the North Bank end, where we had a worm's eye view of his successful conversion.

I don't particularly remember how, when I attended a match, I killed the time between school finishing at 12 noon and the match kicking off at three pm. I know I sometimes sat in West Park, ate my sandwiches and fed the ducks but, on other occasions, I must have been under cover from the rain or warming myself against the cold. What I do know is that it was necessary to be in the ground an hour before kick-off if I wanted a good position of my choosing. Crowds were big in those days.

My sisters have supported Wolves throughout their lives but have not been match attenders to any great extent. My brother, on the other hand, is an avid supporter and has been all over the country in his younger days. He started when he was 13, on the first day of the 1962-63 season and the result was an eight-one win! Today his wife's fragile health prevents him from attending on any but rare occasions. My youngest sister has three sons, two of whom are glory hunters (Liverpool and Manchester United). But the youngest has kept the faith and I had great pleasure in meeting him at the ground in 2014 when 10k went to MK, where he now lives.

I didn't immediately let on to my schoolmates that I had crossed the Rubicon at last and become a true Wolves follower. Why not, you might well ask. Well I had heard them as they discussed matches in very learned fashion and I was painfully aware that my technical knowledge of football tactics, formations and strategies was sadly lacking, in comparison to theirs. I didn't want them asking my views as to why Wolves had failed to beat West Bromwich in the last match, or whether I thought Wilshaw or Mason was the better inside forward. I didn't want to display my complete ignorance. But I was soon rumbled!

The next home match was against Burnley and I paid an early visit to the stadium after school to buy a programme so that I could read it in town whilst eating my lunch. I suddenly became aware of someone running excitedly across the road to intercept me and engage me in conversation.

"Well, you're a dark horse, aren't you? You never told us you went to the matches. I'd never have guessed!"

"I don't," I lied,

"Then why have you just bought a programme?"

The cat was out of the bag and from then onwards I went with my mates, enjoyed their company and learned a lot about football.

And so, for a while I had been a closet supporter, ashamed to own up to my allegiance. What sort of supporter is that? The club would be far better off without people like me! If I was ashamed to own up to it at the beginning, what were the chances of my still being a fan 60 years later? Undoubtedly, they were close to zero. There would never be a chance for me to write an account of my 60 years of supporting Wolves!

Chapter 3
Three Magical Seasons

Where were you back in '57
When Wolves transported us to Heaven?

Perhaps you were a little late
And joined the fun in '58?

Or '59, the season when
We won the FA Cup again?

Whichever year you saw them play
Your memories will always stay.

The three seasons 1957-58, 1958-59 and 1959-60 were the best trio of years and the most magical in the history of Wolverhampton Wanderers. We won the League title twice, the FA Cup once and came within a single point of winning the double of league and cup, and were also one point away from a treble of successive league titles - and I was fortunate enough to be there to witness all this drama as it unfolded!

People often say to me I am an extremely lucky person to have seen the very best Wolves team but, then again, they sympathise with my suffering now as we toil away in the nether regions of the league, perhaps never to reach the pinnacle of success again. It's true, it does hurt to have witnessed the dramatic decline over the years, but time moves on; we are on the way back - of that I am convinced - and I wouldn't have missed those three wonderful years for all the subsequent success I could have enjoyed, had I become a Manchester United, a Liverpool, a Chelsea or an Arsenal fan. Those three wonderful years are indescribable, and etched on my memory, and I have no words to express my thanks for being there then. In fact, only four results in those whole three seasons really stand out and cause me regret now, and they are:

Bolton Wanderers v Wolves 1-2 FA Cup Round 6;
> 1st March 1958 - it probably cost us a double of league and cup.

Nottingham Forest v Wolves 0-0 League;
> 18th April 1960 - it cost us the double, as well as three successive championships.

Wolves v Tottenham Hotspur 1-3 League;
> 23rd April 1960 - ditto.

Wolves v Fulham 9-0 League;
> 16th Sept 1959 - I wasn't there!

Let's look at those four matches one by one:

We were storming it in the cup in that year of 1958, a 1-0 win at Lincoln City in the third round followed by 5-1 and 6-1 hammerings of Portsmouth and Darlington at Molineux in rounds four and five. We went to Bolton in the quarter-finals for what turned out to be the siege of Burnden Park, Bolton somehow holding firm against an absolute battering by Wolves. We pulverised the other Wanderers but were unable to get the ball past flailing bodies, the post, the bar, or heroic goalkeeping, for the equaliser. When it was all over the Wolves fans trudged back home, their tails between their legs, unable to believe Wolves were not through to the semi-finals. I had been listening, aghast, on the radio at home.

It's problematic of course as to whether or not we would have won the double if we had beaten Bolton in the quarter-finals that day, because we still had to win a semi-final and final against, at that time, unknown opponents but when we faced Forest at the City Ground on Easter Tuesday, 1960, having beaten them the day before, by 3-1 at Molineux, a win would subsequently have given us a third successive title (only Huddersfield Town in the 20s and Arsenal in the 30s had achieved that feat so far) and the first league and cup double of the 20th century. But, sadly and frustratingly, we could only manage a 0-0 draw. That dropped point was to prove crucial at the end of the season.

To compound the misery, we lost the next match, at home to Spurs, who went on to win the double themselves the following season. 56,000 fans were crammed into the ground and the South Bank was jammed. It was so full I couldn't get up from the gangway onto the terracing and I didn't see any play at all until the second half, when people moved about a bit, freeing up some space. Supporters had climbed up the gantries of the floodlight pylons to gain superb, if precarious, vantage points.

After those two set-backs we won our last match of the season, 5-1 at Chelsea, and had to sweat it out, while Burnley, who were playing their final match (postponed from earlier in the season) a few days after the official end of the season, were presented with the opportunity of pinching the title from us. They duly managed it, with a 2-1 win against their Lancashire neighbours, Manchester City. Did I say neighbours? Well, that's what they were / are, and they were particularly neighbourly that night, at least as far as the score was concerned.

I am making no accusations of match rigging but, if you were not around in those days, you can only imagine the disappointment and the feeling of being cheated out of the title that pervaded the mood of the Wolves supporters. Why were Burnley allowed to play such a vital match outside the regular season, when they knew exactly what they needed to do to win the title? Today, all final matches of the season are played on the same day and at the same time. If Burnley and Wolves had played their final matches simultaneously - who knows? Burnley might have played it safe and settled for a draw; they couldn't have predicted that we would thrash Chelsea 5-1 away, just days before the Cup Final. It wasn't just any old title we were deprived of. It was a three-in-a-row title and one half of a double bid. It still rankles bitterly today and makes me wish I could wind back the clock to 1960 and see those fixtures played again.

The match against Fulham on 16th September 1959 must go down as one of the all-time great performances, by Wolves or any other team. Unfortunately, it was a midweek match and transport would have been tricky for me, having to stay long hours in Wolverhampton after school and then finding a late-night bus home to Albrighton after the match. As we had lost the corresponding match to them the week before, 1-3 at Craven Cottage, some shine had been taken off the prospect of a good result and I decided to stay at home and concentrate on my A-level homework. In any case, I had broken my elbow a few weeks previously, playing football on the hard fields of a parched 1959 summer, and I still had my arm in plaster. What a match I missed!

In those days, if one was not actually at the game, the result was very hard to discover, particularly if the match in question was a midweek one, played in the evening. No internet was available in those dim days of history, no mobile phone alerts, no Jeff Stelling on Sky Sports to keep one up to date! The only thing to do was to sleep on it and wait to read about it in the newspaper in the morning. Now, I must reveal a very dark secret - my dad was a Spurs supporter!

He disliked my Wolves affiliation and sniped from the side-lines constantly. "Wolves aren't a very good team at all. They are just good at playing the offside game." I don't think he really understood football.

"And anyway," he added, "they'll lose tonight. They were well beaten by Fulham last week. They are two-season wonders, you'll see."

I went to bed that night in trepidation, unable to sleep, as is usually the case when Wolves have played and I don't know the result. I got up at the crack of dawn, determined to intercept the paper before Dad got his hands on it. I needed to come up with a good story, in the event of things having gone horribly wrong. I pulled the paper out of the letterbox. There was no need to open it up. There on the back page, emblazoned in huge characters, was the stunning headline:

WOLVES NINE GOAL WONDERS

Shell-shocked, I read the report nine times, once for each goal, then placed the paper, headline uppermost, on Dad's breakfast-cereal bowl and crept back to bed with a broad smile on my face. Could life be any sweeter?

I don't feel qualified to comment on the match too much as I wasn't there, but I do know that Ron Flowers scored an absolute cracker of a long range shot to set up a 3-0 interval lead, that Norman Deeley couldn't stop scoring and helped himself to four goals and that Bobby Mason missed a last-minute sitter which would have put the score into double figures. The Fulham team, including the late and lamented Jimmy Hill, formed a guard of honour to applaud the Wolves players off the pitch at the final whistle, a great sporting gesture which you would be unlikely to see today.

Incidentally, Deeley scored our solitary goal in the 1-3 defeat at Fulham the previous week. So, in the space of a week, he found the back of Fulham's net five times. He was in the middle of a purple scoring patch, hitting the target 10 times in seven matches.

There were many more fabulous highlights in that fabulous trio of years and I will describe some of those that I remember in the next chapter.

Chapter 4
1957-60 continued

We won the league once and we won it again
No possible reason to carp or complain.
In 59-60 we partly slipped up
By missing the league but then winning the Cup.

In that fabulous first season of watching Wolves I didn't see them lose until Arsenal beat them 1-2 on Easter Tuesday (we seemed to have trouble with Easter Tuesday matches, for some reason). In fact, that was the only home match we lost all season, finishing the campaign with a magnificent home record of W17, D3, L1 - in stark contrast to the 2016-17 season just finished when we lost at home no fewer than 11 times. We are in a different league now, quite literally. There are quite a few highlights I can still recall from that season of 1957-58 without having to refer to records:

I remember a piece of magic from Norman Deeley on a cold December afternoon, just before Christmas, in a match against Everton. Some sage standing near me opined loudly to those around him that "Norman Deeley hasn't got a football brain." A hostage to fortune if ever there was one, and total rubbish to boot! No sooner had he said this than the brainless Deeley, receiving the ball close to the touchline, took it in his stride, cutting diagonally inside one defender, then cutting diagonally inside another defender, taking him in a zig-zag progression to about the central point of Everton's half of the field. He then slid the ball forward onto Jimmy Mullen's left foot. Well, anyone who has seen Mullen with the ball on his left foot within sight of goal knows there will be only one outcome; "one-nil", as David Coleman would have said. Not bad for a footballer who was lacking a brain!

Another thoroughly enjoyable match that season was the fixture against Birmingham City on 22nd February. I remember it vividly: Deeley popped up in front of goal early on, and we were quickly in front; Murray then materialised in a similar position and it was 2-0; Deeley was there again for 3-0; Murray scored another to make it 4-0; and then Jimmy Murray completed a fine and rapid hat-trick - 5-0, and it was only half-time! Unfortunately, we took our foot off the gas in the second half, scored no more goals and the final score was 5-1, but it was the second time that season we had turned our local rivals over by that 5-1 score-line.

This excellent form carried on, week after week throughout the season, until the title decider against Preston North End came up on 19th April. Preston had been chasing us gallantly, but with little hope, for some months. Every time they won we did too and they couldn't close the gap. Wolves beat Preston 2-0 that day, with a goal from Deeley, together with Milne's own goal, and opened the floodgates to joyful celebrations. I remember little about the actual match, apart from admiring the great Tom Finney, who was unable to conjure up anything for his team on that day. I do remember spilling onto the pitch, that had become a heaving mass of humanity, to greet the players, who showed off the trophy from the Waterloo Road stand.

We had 62 points and needed four more from the last two matches, both of which were away, to equal the league record. We thrashed the post-Munich Busby Babes 4-0 at Old Trafford but we then came a cropper in the final match, losing 1-2 to already-relegated Sheffield Wednesday. Even the great teams switch off from time to time when the season is close to ending and holidays beckon. Human nature hasn't changed over the past 60 years and it probably never will. It just seems that, back in those times, the players cared a little more than they do now and had more of a genuine commitment to their club and to the fans than do some of today's mercenaries.

Let me just say a word about Manchester United. No greater tragedy has ever befallen an English football team than the disaster that was the Munich air crash, when so many young lives were so tragically lost, but this disaster has been used unfairly by some critics to detract from Wolves' great successes of the late 50s. Wolves had already defeated United 3-1 on 28th September 1957, ten matches into the campaign, and were well ahead of them in February, before the disaster occurred. We had also beaten the mighty and all-conquering Real Madrid, 3-2 at Molineux, in a floodlit friendly match earlier in the season. Although we grieved at United's terrible losses we were the better team that year and were worthy champions.

Season 1958-59 started with a rush of goals, not all of them in our opponents' nets, it needs to be said. The new campaign started well enough with a 5-1 trouncing of Forest at Molineux (I don't remember any details of the goals, although there was a rare hat-trick from Bobby Mason), but there quickly followed two pointless trips to London, a 0-2 defeat at West Ham United's Upton Park, followed by a 2-6 thrashing at Stamford Bridge by Chelsea, the young Jimmy Greaves helping himself to five goals and, by all reports, giving Billy Wright the run around. In the first ten matches, we scored 21 goals and conceded 17, picking up 11 points and dropping nine. It was probably inevitable that we would be prematurely written off by the pundits, and for Wright to be declared past it, but a strong Christmas, followed by 11 wins and two draws in the last 13 matches, kept the trophy securely at Molineux for the third occasion overall and the second time in successive seasons.

Christmas 1958 saw an incredible double-header against Portsmouth. In those days, the same opponents were taken on, home and away, over a period of two or three days at the Christmas and Easter holiday periods. On Boxing Day Wolves won 5-3 at Fratton Park and the following day ran riot, with a 7-0 victory at Molineux. Peter Broadbent, being tried experimentally as a centre forward, scored a hat-trick at Fratton, while Norman Deeley and Colin Booth did likewise in the Molineux match, both Deeley and Booth helping themselves to four goals each over the two matches. I was there for the seven-nil trouncing and it was a great Christmas present, with little hint of the carnage to come as the teams went in at half time, with Wolves holding a narrow one-nil lead. But, just as in the Fulham 9-0 win the following season, Wolves blitzed six goals in the second half.

I think players were hardier in those days. Matches on successive days over the holiday periods didn't seem to trouble them too much, even although there weren't massive squad rotations available to ease the strain of Easter Monday and Easter Tuesday matches, for instance. But I digress.

Before the Christmas just described, however, on a murky, foggy day in November I travelled on the slow train to Burnley for my first ever away match. It seemed as if we would never arrive, as the train, its smoke contributing to the poor visibility, trundled through the murky wastes of the Lancashire moors, the scenery almost obliterated by the dense fog. The Turf Moor floodlights were on throughout the afternoon, as I took up my station along the side of the pitch, in what we then called the Enclosure area.

From the start, we came under quite a bit of heavy pressure as Burnley went for the jugular, but Wright and co held firm. Half way through the first half Norman Deeley, who had been hugging the touchline near me and not involved much in the action, received the ball to feet. In trademark style, he took the ball in his stride inside the full back and floated a beautiful lofted cross into the box. It was met by young debutant, Alan Jackson, with a glorious soaring header and Wolves were one up, somewhat against the run of play.

The Burnley assault continued in the second half but again the defence stood firm. When it seemed that we must crack under the pressure, Des Horne eased the situation by breaking away down the left channel and finding Deeley, in the right place at the right time to do the other thing he did so well, tucking the ball into the net from a position in front of the goal; two-nil and it was game over.

On Burnley railway station after the match an older local fan said to gold-and-black-clad me: "Well, Billy Wright is past it now, isn't he?" I don't know how he worked that one out, since Wright had superbly marshalled his defence to repel a ferocious aerial bombardment from Burnley, and had kept a clean sheet into the bargain.

After Christmas, we suffered our regulation Cup exit against Bolton, this time at home. We gave them the usual pummelling but got bogged down in the Molineux mud. A golden chance to equalise fell to Deeley near the end of the match - he stretched for the ball and, unable to get any power on the shot, he toe-poked it from about three yards out, but the ball just trickled a few inches and stuck stubbornly in the glutinous slime. The Molineux pitch wasn't always in prime condition in those days, and certainly not in mid-winter.

Back in the league, Manchester United and Arsenal were chasing us hard, and both had turns at heading the table. We lost a fantastic match 1-2 at Old Trafford in February, with the young Bobby Charlton excelling. Arsenal came to town two weeks later and the London press were eagerly sharpening their pencils at the prospect of the Gunners getting the better of us. It was with supreme delight that, having accompanied an Arsenal supporter from school into the Molineux Street Enclosure for the eagerly awaited match, I saw Wolves dissect Arsenal to the tune of 6-1! The Broadbent / Deeley partnership, operating on the left this time, did the main damage, the duo scoring two goals apiece. Micky Lill, a rising star, played on the right wing that day and he also scored a goal. In 18 matches that season he scored 12 goals from the wing, including a hat-trick against West Bromwich Albion, but his career at Wolves was short-lived.

I attended my second away match, closer to home than Burnley and on a much clearer day, when I visited St Andrew's, home of local rivals Birmingham City, to witness a thoroughly workmanlike and dominant three-nil win. Leading up to one of the goals, Broadbent paused, teasing the full back before sending him the wrong way with a devastating body swerve, and then sprinting to the by-line and pulling the ball back onto Jimmy Murray's head. Putting the ball on Murray's head in front of goal usually had the same effect as placing it on Jimmy Mullen's left foot in a similar position.

"Pooh!" scoffed a Bluenose supporter near me, "They've got no skill; they're just fast." Did he expect Peter to perform his body swerve and his run to the line slowly so that Birmingham had time to block his cross? Did he suppose that anything executed at speed couldn't be equally skilful?

The second successive title was wrapped up with a swashbuckling 5-0 slaughter of Luton Town at Molineux, in which Peter Broadbent scored one of the finest headed goals I have seen in my 60 years of watching football. Somebody crossed the ball to around the penalty spot, PB rose, hung in the air, pulled his head back and then whipped it forward like a rebounding punch-ball. As he made full contact with his forehead he flexed his neck muscles, turned his head and directed the ball into the top corner of the net. No flick header this - it was a full-on, directed header at full force, with Broadbent seeming to hang in the air whilst he executed it.

And so, for the second successive year, we cavorted on the pitch.

A sad but inevitable event occurred at the beginning of the new season (1959-60) when the great Billy Wright announced his retirement as a footballer. His had been a great and illustrious career, underwritten by impeccable conduct and a record of never having been cautioned. He was given a great send off in the pre-season practice match (Whites against the Colours), after which he handed over the centre half role, first to George Showell and Eddie Stuart, and then to the cultured Bill Slater.

Season 1959-60 started with even more goals than did the previous season. In the first 10 matches 47 goals were scored, 30 for us and 17 for the opposition. Included in this goal fest were the 9-0 Fulham win, already described, and a 6-4 thriller at Maine Road, where the score oscillated back and forth in dramatic fashion. Bill Slater, substituting for the injured Peter Broadbent in an unaccustomed role for him of inside forward, demonstrated his versatility and skill by scoring twice to help Wolves win. The score progression (home team first) was 1-0, 2-0, 2-1, 2-2, 2-3, 3-3, 3-4 and half-time! Then it carried on 4-4, 4-5, 4-6, the scoring ceasing at the 67-minute mark. And, just to add to these goal blitzes, there followed in the next seven matches the 9-0 Fulham result and a 5-1 win over Luton but, more disturbingly, a 1-5 reverse at Tottenham, the latter an ominous portent of things to come in the not-too-distant future.

Burnley were the team to beat, and beat them we did in magnificent style in a mid-week match in March. 6-1 was the score and all five forwards got their names on the scoresheet. This made it all-the-more galling when, a few weeks later, Burnley sneaked up on the rails to pip us to the title.

I've already described the torment of losing the title to Burnley after the season proper had ended. I think the London-loving press were willing and praying for Wolves to fail: a third successive title for only the third time ever in the history of the football league and a possible first double of the century, with a Cup Final appearance on the horizon, was too much for them to contemplate from a Midlands team. Wolves failed in their historic bid and, my word, didn't London snap up the chance to put it out of their reach for ever! Tottenham became the "Glory, Glory, Hallelujah" team of the century, and everybody's darlings, when it could so easily have been Wolves.

But it was the FA Cup which brought glory to us that season. We landed a tough tie in the third round, away to Newcastle United, but survived with an excellent 2-2 draw at St James's Park, both wing halves, Clamp and Flowers, scoring. The replay on a snow-covered Molineux pitch saw us play some of our best football of the competition as Wolves went through by four goals to two, Ron Flowers again scoring.

I was at that match, and was also at the fourth-round tie versus Charlton Athletic. It was raining and very muddy and, coupled with a superb display of defiance from Willie Duff in the visitors' goal, it turned out to be the hardest match of the competition. Broadbent eventually managed to get his header to plop over the line when it looked as though Charlton would hold out at one-one for a replay.

Away victories followed at Luton Town and Leicester City and then I was off to the Hawthorns for the Semi-Final against Aston Villa. Norman Deeley scored the only goal of a very tight match and we were through to the final and a day out at Wembley!

It was Deeley again who took the plaudits in the final, with two goals, while Wolves were unfairly booed for alleged foul play, an emotional response to the unfortunate fracture that Blackburn's Dave Whelan suffered to his leg. The least said about the scurrilous accusations made against Norman Deeley after his death, the better. Deeley was a gentleman, who played enthusiastically but fairly and would never intentionally have injured another player. The unfairness in branding him a malicious leg-breaker, when he couldn't defend himself from beyond the grave, was beneath contempt.

Just a word about Bill Slater, the most cultured centre half I have seen. He won the Player of the Year award in 1960, and the sight of him dribbling the ball out of defence was a joy to behold. He was a ball-playing centre half, almost as skilful as Broadbent with his feet, and far -removed from some of the hoofers we often see today. If Wolves were in trouble he wouldn't belt the ball into touch or lump it high down the field. Instead, he would win the ball, dribble it out as if it were magnetised to his boots, emerge into space and pass constructively to a nearby colleague in attendance. He was a thinking man's central defender.

What a wonderful memory with which to end my account of those wonderful three years.

Chapter 5
Running Away from It All

My football friends can't see the fun
in going for a training run.
They say "You must be off your rocker,
if you like running more than soccer!"

Why don't you come and watch the game?
In contrast, running's very tame.
You'll only trip and fall down holes;
At Molineux, you'll see some goals.

My athletics career got off to humble beginnings at school. Every year on Sports Day there was a whole-school one-mile race, in which boys from all years could take part, although participation was entirely optional. I think this was designed to build character and determination and the ability to accept defeat, because the younger lads had no chance of finishing ahead of their upper school superiors and they would experience what it was to be beaten, for sure.

I don't remember if it was in Form I or Form II (Year Seven or Year Eight in today's terms) when I first decided to give the race a try. Anyway, I gave it my best shot, but still finished a good last. Everybody was very sympathetic and patronising: "Well done. It's the taking part that counts, you know."

This wasn't the greatest of encouragements to spur me on to pursue a future running career, but a subsequent PE lesson, in which we ran races in groups of five or six over 50 metres and in which I won my race, excited me and I competed in the school mile every year from then on. In Form V (year 11) I was improving quite a lot and, on Sports Day, having let the champion get almost a lap in front of me (the track was 220 yards, and so it was eight laps to the mile), I hauled him back to about 50 yards, but he held on, with a few worried looks over his shoulder, to win the title once again. He had now won it two years in succession.

After the race the champion, who was a year older than me, came over to speak to me: "Let me give you a tip, young man; don't let the leader get so far ahead. You'll never catch him up again" - the patronising creep! But there was always next year to try again and to pull him down a peg or two.

Next year came around, and, as in previous years, I trained with Mr Champion round the school playing fields at lunch time in preparation for the big race. He liked to train with me so that he could psyche me out, by showing me who was the stronger runner and certain to prevail on Sports Day. He used a particularly tough routine, known as Fartlek, which was originated by the great Finnish runner, Paavo Nurmi, in which the pace is increased from a slow jog to flat out speed for anything up to 300 metres, before easing back down to a jog recovery and then winding back up again to full throttle. In earlier years this had killed me off, but not so this time. I was a year older and a year fitter and a year more determined to give him his comeuppance.

He wound up the pace for 50 metres and I stayed with him. We recovered with a jog and then he wound it up again, this time to a lung-bursting 100 metres - I stayed with him again and he looked surprised, not to say a little worried. Once more he tried it - and again I was still there. "That was a good session," I remarked breezily, although feeling shattered, as we warmed down. I never saw him again. He had finished his exams and didn't show his face at school again. Mr Champion knew he was beaten and had chickened out.

In the school sports that year I won the School Mile and the 880 yards. I had to make up a deficit to win the mile and, apparently, some workers on the roof of one of the nearby school buildings were banging with their shovels and hammers as I closed the gap.

These performances greatly encouraged me and I was further encouraged by the presence of two watching coaches from Wolverhampton & Bilston Athletic Club who congratulated me and told me I should take up the sport. I did, but not for several more years.

Our family had now moved to Stone and I continued to study at St Chad's College, travelling in by train each day and continuing to attend most Wolves home matches. I remember that, when I needed to book an advance ticket for a match in the school holidays, such as a cup tie, I would cycle from Stone to Wolverhampton, along the A34 and the A449, collect the ticket and cycle back home again, a round trip of 50 miles. At least there was a good cycle track to ride on along the A449.

When I left school, I began work in chemical laboratories near Stone and started to play in a table tennis league - which made midweek football matches difficult to attend at times. I was also doing training runs quite regularly and eventually felt the need to join a running club. That was a further nail in the Molineux attendance coffin, as most races fell on Saturday afternoons. However, despite this, I did have a good Wolves attendance record throughout the 1960s; it was only when I was elected team manager for my club in the mid-1970s that I became a less regular attender.

I began to run marathons in a big way in the early 1980s and discovered that I was quite good at them. The commitment required to train for such a punishing event left little time for other pursuits, and the strain on the legs incurred by standing at a football match for two hours or more was very arduous and challenging, when marathon training was making itself felt in the muscles and joints. Around this time, I married my darling wife at the venerable age of 40 (she was 29) and we were blessed with two wonderful daughters, both of whom are Wolves supporters, but distant ones because of where they now live.

I picked up a real prize in my wife. Not only is she 11 years younger than me, a delightful woman and the love of my life, but she is also the former British Marathon record holder. In 1976 the ladies British record stood at three hours and nine minutes. In a ladies-only race around the perimeter of Heathrow

Airport on Good Friday, 1976, my not-then wife smashed the record by an incredible 18 minutes and became the first British woman to dip under three hours - she ran 2 hours, 50 minutes and 55 seconds and earned an entry in the Guinness Book of Records! The following year someone beat her record by one second, well within the margin of error for timekeeping over almost three hours but, in any case, my wife will forever hold the title of first British woman to run under three hours, just as Sir Roger Bannister will always be the first man to have cracked four minutes for the mile. She has been my rock and my life and now supports me lovingly through my Parkinson's difficulties.

We got together through athletics. In August of 1981 I took a party of teenage boys and girls for a week's training on the sand dunes of Merthyr Mawr, near Porthcawl in South Wales, reputed to be the highest dunes in Europe. My future wife, as a teacher, accompanied me to help maintain order. And boy, did I need help to control those rebellious teenagers, and she provided that in abundance. It later transpired that these young people, so-called athletes, had signed up for the training camp not to train but to have a good time. (One of the youths had a not-so-good time, sleeping out under the stars on a chill night, as I threw him and his sleeping-bag out of the house). Three months after the training camp, on my 40th birthday, we announced our engagement and I received lots of good wishes from the young scoundrels with whom I had been at loggerheads on the training camp. The following summer we were married. But let's return to my own running.

In 1984, I ran my career best marathon of two hours, thirty-two minutes and fifty-one seconds, appropriately enough on the roads in and around Wolverhampton. Our first daughter had been born five days previously and it was strange and very gratifying to hear bystanders shouting out "Come on Dad!" It became a Pavlovian response to respond whenever the word "dad" was shouted out.

I continued to run marathons on into the 1990s but by then I was slowing down slowly but relentlessly, as most runners do when they reach their 50s.

I gave up marathons when I reached 50 years of age in 1991 but continued to compete in cross-country, which I enjoyed as much as any branch of the sport. However, my performances were anything but satisfying and I steadily drifted towards the back of the field. I was baffled, as I still had the same fighting and competitive spirit as previously, but my body wouldn't seem to do what was asked of it. Looking back now, it is clear what was going on; Parkinson's was setting in.

Parkinson's is a neurological degenerative disease in which the brain's dopamine neurons, responsible for movement and locomotion, are depleted and die. By the time the condition has been diagnosed in an individual, up to 80% of the neurons have already been lost. I was diagnosed in 2007, which means that, during the late 90s and early years of the new millennium, Parkinson's was there, behind the scenes, doing its evil work undetected. No wonder running was now so difficult for me. I gave it up in 2006, but dabbled with it again a few years later (see Chapter 24).

However, it wasn't all couch potato stuff in the noughties. Between 2004 and 2007 I tackled Mt Kilimanjaro in Tanzania three times. The first time I think I overdosed on anti-altitude-sickness tablets and collapsed in the snow at 18,500 feet, just 800 feet below the summit.

On the second occasion, I felt magnificent and was going great guns when I slipped in a gully and twisted my knee at 16,000 feet, forcing me to retire. I was stepping aside to make room for a heavily-laden porter who was descending the track when I slipped - so much for good manners and consideration for the convenience of other people!

And on the third and final attempt my Parkinson's was really making itself felt as I stumbled and swayed and staggered up to 9,000 feet, where I had to admit defeat and withdraw reluctantly.

And so, my mountaineering days were sadly over, but I said goodbye to the magnificent mountain that was Kilimanjaro with no regrets and some very fond memories.

We climbed the mountain the first time in aid of the Anthony Nolan Trust for bone marrow donors, to give a life chance to leukaemia sufferers; 17 of us bonded into a close-knit group and when we returned home we held a party for one of our number's 50th birthday. The poem that follows is what I read out to the assembled throng:

Although I dance the hokey-kokey
I am no good at karaoke,
And so, I thought I could do worse
Than entertain you all in verse.

I want to speak of Tanzania
Where most of us supped Tusker beer,
Then undertook a trek most hilly
upon the mountain known as 'Kili'.

We all were there: him, her and me,
to fund raise for the A.N.T.
A worthy cause; through toil and strife,
We hoped to bring to others - life.

But it was not a solemn climb;
For fun and friendship, we found time.
We started mad and then got dafter,
with Taffy's pranks and Graham's laughter.

The brothers Grimm, two Chelsea boys,
Could both make quite a lot of noise
When talking football - it got boring,
But even worse was Tony's snoring.

A business deal Paul did not bungle
as we went strolling through the jungle.
Fresh coffee beans, both whole and ground,
would cost just 80 cents a pound.

The jeep drove high and we were shaking
And all our teeth and bones were quaking.
But it was worth the bumpy ride

I LOVE TO GO A WANDERING

when several village schools we spied.

Computer tasks within the school
Young Emma couldn't do at all.
If she returns the kiddies might
Just show her how to get them right.

As we descended from the church
Banana beer made Tony lurch.
Then back at base it was high time
We all got ready for the climb.

The kit inspection in the chalet
Caused loads of grief to Yve and Annie.
They couldn't move around at all
As Emma's kit spread wall to wall.

The final packing was quite hard,
And then we gathered in the yard
To get bags weighed and meet our porter
And fill each platypus with water.

The first day's climb was led by Tony,
Careering up on Shanks's pony,
So he could stop and shed his bag,
Then craftily roll out a fag.

Though they'd sore feet we couldn't carry
the limping brothers, Paul and Gary.
And then we all went into hoots;
They each had on the other's boots!

Now Annie got on very well
with Gibson's dad, Emmanuel.

On each occasion, she saw Papa
She greeted him with "Hallelujah!"

We faced a simply huge dilemma
in finding storage room for Emma.
No way was just one mountain bunk
sufficient space for all her junk.

When things got tough enough to peeve
Our generally placid Yve,
The word from Emma's stand-in mother
Did sound suspiciously like 'bugrrr!'

Above Mandara we lost Dean
But then he came back - "where've you been?"
Our Taffy grinned from ear to ear,
"It's copious and very clear!"

Now Graham sat upon the throne;
He wouldn't have if he had known.
An angry fraulein called him names;
"Come out! Those ones are for the dames."

Not one of us, if we could choose,
would use the dreaded long-drop loos.
But in the middle of the night
Two trekkers went out for a ... sight ...

... of moon and stars and Milky Way;
all putting on a grand display.
The constellations that they saw
Just made the trekkers gaze in awe.

At Kibo Huts we weren't too posh

I LOVE TO GO A WANDERING

To worry that we couldn't wash,
Although it greatly bothered Annie
She couldn't clean her teeth - poor granny!

On summit night we wrapped up warm,
And just as well, for what a storm!
Three reached Uhuru and the rest
The ridge at Gillman's Point did crest.

On Gillman's all the gents and ladies
Considered it as bad as Hades,
Except for one who lay below,
Collapsed and lying in the snow.

Retracing steps, the big man Shaw
Was feeling pretty bruised and sore;
For, down the scree at break of dawn,
crashed eighteen stone of Scottish brawn.

Another Scot, James, didn't care
For genteel language - he could swear.
His tone was nothing short of mocking
when someone said, "The weather's shocking".

The third Scot, Alec, was distraught;
The pocket camera that he'd brought
Fell in the snow drifts out of sight;
to spoil an otherwise great night.

But his emotions turned full cycle,
When, later on, he spoke to Michael.
The TV man with eyes so keen
His camera in the snow had seen.

On Friday in the afternoon
It changed from blizzard to monsoon.
Our feet and hands and bums were soaking.
I do assure you I'm not joking.

But, nothing daunted, we weren't late
In racing downwards to the gate,
Where, from the pockets of our coats,
We paid for drinks with soggy notes.

At base camp it was party night,
But compere Ian had a fright.
The lady fixed him with a glare;
He'd gone and bust her favourite chair.

Daniel and Catherine looked besotted.
The reason was they'd just got knotted.
Then, though she tried with all her might,
Her jeans, alas, were just too tight

... to let her gather with her teeth
the spoon enticingly beneath.
The helpful watchers thought she should
Remove the jeans - as if she would!

And so to bed, to sleep and dream
Of all the things we'd done and seen.
Then Saturday we caught the plane
which took us all back home again.

This almost finishes my saga
of mountains, forests, beer and lager.
It hasn't been a tale of woe,

I LOVE TO GO A WANDERING

despite torrential rain and snow.

And so, to end, you will agree
This party's just the place to be.
Now let's all say, before we leave;
"A very happy birthday, Yve."

Chapter 6
Four in a Row

For four successive seasons, we produced a magic ton.

Jim Murray, Broadbent and Norman Deeley scored two-two-five,

One hundred and two, and sixty-two, and sixty-one;

This magnificent scoring trio brought the ground alive.

.

By scoring 103, 110, 106 and 103 goals respectively in the four consecutive seasons 1957-58, 1958-59, 1959-60 and 1960-61 Wolves set a league record that has not been bettered since. And, with only 38 games now played in the top division, compared with the 42 in the days of Wolves' pomp, it is unlikely ever to be equalled. It's true that 46 games are played in the lower divisions, and one might think it could be beaten there. But any team scoring a century of goals in a lower division is very likely to be promoted and, in the tougher competition of the higher divisions, would then be very unlikely to score one hundred goals the next season, and certainly not the season after that and then the season after that again. And so, I confidently predict that Wolves' record of four successive league centuries will last forever.

Incidentally, there is a quite amazing record that Wolves don't hold and, what is more, would probably prefer not to. In season 1957-58 Manchester City scored 104 goals (one more than Wolves did), but they failed to win honours because they conceded 100! They may be the only team in history to have a century of goals recorded in both the 'F' and the 'A' columns. The Wolves v Man City matches were certainly high-scoring affairs that season, Wolves drawing 3-3 at Molineux and winning 4-3 at Maine Road. Their brilliant attack and shocking defence saw City finish in 5th place that season.

Wolves' achievement of quadruple centuries is quite incredible, particularly as, in 1960-61, the Wolves decline, though slight, had already commenced. They had slipped from 1st to 2nd and then down to 3rd in successive seasons (and the following year they would end up in a worrying 18th position, finishing four points clear of relegation, admittedly with a superior goal average to the two relegated teams). What is even more incredible is that just three players scored 225 of the 422 goals amassed in those four 'ton-up' seasons. Jimmy Murray netted 102, Peter Broadbent accumulated 62 and Norman Deeley scored 61 times. The remaining 47% of the goals scored in those four seasons came from 18 different players (together with nine own goals from helpful opponents).

Deeley's achievement was remarkable for a winger, and particularly impressive were the 23 goals he poached in 1957-58. Broadbent showed what a good goal scorer he was, in addition to his main role of genius and playmaker, while Murray often went unnoticed but was a crucial part of Wolves' success. He was a slightly-built striker but was a devastatingly consistent scorer.

It was sad that we won nothing in that fourth ton season, after three years of abundance. Our defence of the FA Cup petered out in a whimper, as we lost to Huddersfield Town in the third round after a replay. The league season started well enough, five wins coming from the first six matches, but then we went seven matches with just one solitary win. The newly dominant Tottenham Hotspur team, superbly managed by Bill Nicholson, were in the process of winning their opening eleven matches, the eleventh being a 4-0 crushing of ourselves at Molineux. A new era had dawned.

We plodded on through the season, mixing good and bad results, and finishing our away programme with a fine 5-1 win at Arsenal, hope perhaps for the next season. One ray of sunshine was the emergence of a new centre forward talent - young Ted Farmer scored 28 goals in 27 appearances. However, Ted suffered a bad injury and hardly figured the following season.

A rather infamous incident concerning Farmer occurred on All-Fools day, 1961, in a match against Manchester City. Wolves had been battling hard to break down the City defence but were constantly denied by the brilliance of Bert Trautmann in the City goal. When it looked as though Wolves would have to settle for a 0-0 draw a cross came in from the left, which Jimmy Murray met with one of his unstoppable headers. Words must have been exchanged earlier between Bert and Ted because the reaction of the young Wolves striker to Murray's goal was to bend over the prone and beaten goalie and clap him in a jeering and mocking manner. It was quite disgraceful behaviour by Farmer and reports suggest he received an outraged reprimand from his boss, Stan Cullis, after the match.

Season 1961-62 was a considerable shock, with Wolves dicing with relegation for the first time in ten years, but they managed to survive and we all breathed a sigh of relief. One more decent season followed in 1962-63, but relegation wasn't far away. It duly struck two years later.

That season of 1962-63 started incredibly well, with eight wins and three draws in the opening 11 matches, better even than we had achieved in any of our three championship seasons in the previous decade. We won our first five away matches, a club record which still stands, including victories at the homes of the two previous champions, Spurs and Ipswich Town, but it didn't last - there was then no win in the next seven games.

Stan Cullis went for youth in a big way from the start of that season, with just defender, George Showell, captain Ron Flowers and striker, Jimmy Murray, as the old heads steadying the ship; Fred Davies, Bobby Thomson, Freddie Goodwin, David Woodfield, Terry Wharton, Chris Crowe, Ted Farmer and Alan Hinton made up the young and hungry brigade. The first match saw us wallop Manchester City 8-1 with Ted Farmer, back in the saddle after injury, plundering four. I was present for this one, unlike my absence from the 9-0 Fulham match, previously lamented! My brother was there too, for his first Wolves match. What a one to start with!

Farmer scored two more goals in the next match, a 4-1 win at West Ham United, and he totalled nine goals in just 13 appearances before being struck down with an eventual career-ending injury. And so, over the course of a decade, Wolves had lost two peerless strikers, Roy Swinbourne and Ted Farmer, their careers cruelly curtailed by injury. Wolves won the third match of the season, 2-0 at Blackpool, before dropping their first point in the West Ham return match, the score remaining nil-nil right up to the referee's final whistle.

The season ebbed and flowed and we finally finished a creditable 5th, with a very good total of 93 goals.

The next season we finished 16th and the season after that (1964-65) Stan Cullis was sacked and Wolves were relegated to the 2nd division. The glory days had well and truly come to an end.

Chapter 7
Nothing for 57 Years

There's many a slip 'twixt the Cup and the lip,
And since that Cup win we've had more than a blip.

We need to move on and there's no going back
past that terrible time when our Stan got the sack.

if there's goodness in life and if there's any justice,
Stan would have remained as the gaffer in harness.

My wife and I have not long returned from our holiday on the beautiful Balearic island of Menorca, where we were stunned by the ruins of ancient stone monuments and settlements, some reputed to be three-thousand years old or more, and many in an excellent state of preservation. So, by my reckoning, the best-preserved village on the island (named Torre D'en Gaumes) was completed by the ancient Menorcan people by the end of the 1000-999 BC season and probably won them the Championship of the Menorcan Stonemasons' League. This is a little before Wolves last won a major trophy (the FA Cup, in 1960) but it feels as if three millennia or more have elapsed since our team last presented us with any silverware.

For, if you discount the Football League Cup, which has borne more sponsors' names than anyone can remember (do you know what it's called now? Do you know what it was called in 1974 and in 1980, the years in which Wolves won it?), Wolves have won no major trophy for 57 years, from the FA Cup win in 1960 to the time of my writing this in 2017. You might well ask why we should discount the League Cup as unworthy of mention. Well, it wasn't taken seriously in its early years, with many of the leading teams not entering the competition for several seasons, and it isn't taken seriously now by some of the top teams, who often field reserve sides against lower-league opposition. True, we have won it twice and I will describe in a later chapter that wonderful day, when I stood on the Wembley terraces in 1974. But, of the truly major trophies, I repeat: we have won nothing for 57 years.

I remember that sad day in 1965 when relegation became a reality. The next day's paper carried a lament to a once great team and told of how "a town and a community had died". How could a team sink in five short years from the heights of winning the FA Cup, and almost winning the double, to the depths of relegation into the 2nd division?

I don't know the answer and I'm not going to speculate in idle conspiracy theories, as I'm not privy to the machinations that went on behind the scenes and in the boardroom, but there must have been some deficiency in planning for the succession. Players wear out, move on and retire, and managers do likewise. Were the club prepared for the departures of Wright and Mullen, Deeley and Broadbent, Slater and Finlayson over a span of not so many years, and did they have their successors lined up? Cullis went bigtime for youth in 1962-63, but when the chips were down the lads couldn't sustain the effort. Did the board invest enough in ready-made, mature replacements? Spurs and other teams were investing heavily in the transfer market, while Wolves were sadly left behind, in the culture of the 50s with only their memories to sustain them.

Had the board given consideration as to whom Cullis's eventual successor might be? If they had, there might have been an easier transition and less of an unjust hatchet job, as the sacking was perceived to be by the Wolves community and by the wider public. These days, such a sacking would be considered normal and inevitable after relegation, but, back in the 60s, it was savage, unreasonable and inexplicable. "You gave your life's blood to Wolves," is a paraphrase of how the great Matt Busby put it to Cullis. In any case, relegation was by no means a certainty at the time of the sacking, so the board's action seems particularly premature and savage. Did they want him out under any pretext?

Fulham's Johnny Haynes had not long won his High Court case, abolishing the £20 a week maximum wage and allowing players to look around for lucrative offers. I remember Ron Flowers, the club skipper, putting in a transfer request and shocking the fans, but I don't recall exactly when it was. If it was around the time of Cullis's sacking the board, under the chairmanship of John Ireland, might have used

Flowers' request as evidence of unrest in the dressing room, and used it as an excuse for the sacking, citing as their justification the fact that he had lost the confidence of the players.

Whatever their reason might have been for sacking Stan Cullis, it was disgraceful in its execution. No public thanks were offered for his 30 years of sterling service and for his quintet of major trophies - he was simply summarily dismissed, like a junior clerk caught with his hand in the till.

Whatever the rights and wrongs of the sacking might have been, there is an apocryphal story that, if true, sticks in my throat and disgusts me. If the rumours are true that Stan Cullis, the greatest manager Wolves, or any club, ever had, was forced after his dismissal to pay at the turnstiles to enter the ground and stand on the terraces, then that enormity is one of the greatest acts of breath-taking ingratitude and injustice ever perpetrated against a good and honest man.

Thankfully his memory is now revered at Molineux, where both a stand and a statue commemorate his name, in splendid solidarity with the great Billy Wright. Cullis and Wright - they are, and always will be, the epitome of Wolves and the standard against which all else is measured.

This unhappy saga is evidence that Wolves, the club, is greater than any player, greater than any manager, greater than any board of directors and greater than any chairman. Supporters continued to attend Molineux (although in much reduced numbers) despite outrage and disgust over the actions of, possibly, one man. And they continued to attend because Wolves was their collective club and not John Ireland's, nor even Stan Cullis's or Billy Wright's.

In the 52 years since their relegation in 1965 Wolves have returned to the top division and been relegated again no fewer than five times. We await the sixth and, we hope, the final promotion with bated breath and with keen anticipation. It must happen soon, mustn't it? I surely can't reach my 70th anniversary of supporting this great club without us finally being established back again in the top flight? These intervening promotions, mostly title wins, were celebrated with great joy at the time, but, somehow, it wasn't the real thing, and it didn't feel like it either. A once great club was struggling, for the most part, in the lower tiers of football, when its rightful place should have been at the top level.

Wolves were footballing pioneers in the 1950s and well ahead of their time, taking the plunge into Europe before anyone else saw the need to do so, and covering themselves in glory in the floodlit friendlies, as they beat the cream of Europe before an avid TV audience. Sadly, in these times when anything that is not Premier League counts for nothing, their record has been pretty-well airbrushed from history. I remember talking to Paul, one of the so-called "Grimm" brothers, on our first Kilimanjaro trip. He and his brother are avid Chelsea supporters (I won't go so far as to accuse them of being band-waggon jumpers!). He was amazed when I told him that Wolves were, at one time, the top team in the land. "It was well before you were a twinkle in your dad's eye, Paul," I told him, "and well before Roman Abramovich was complaining to his dad that he wasn't getting enough pocket money to make ends meet."

Writing this in 2017, many years after the glory times, it has shocked me to realise how short a time that glory lasted and how rapidly the decline took hold. It had seemed, before I wrote this book, that we had been the top team almost for ever. Something went so badly wrong.

If the truth were known, however, it is the case that from the late 1930s up to and including the glory days from 1954 onwards, Wolves were an excellent team, hovering near the top for a quarter of a century. From season 1936-37 up to season 1960-61 they finished 1st three times, 2nd five times, 3rd four times, 5th twice and 6th twice. The only two seasons when they were below par were 1950-51 and 1951-52 when they finished 14th and 16th respectively. That quarter century comprised only 18 seasons because of the intervening world war. It is apparent, therefore, that the actual glory years, from winning their first championship in 1954 up to lifting the FA Cup for the 4th time in 1960, were comparatively short-lived, but they were knocking on the door for a good time before that.

Regrets and sadness are inevitable consequences of following a football team with all your heart, particularly if that team is Wolverhampton Wanderers. But I am not going to dwell on hard times in the rest of this book. Instead, I will describe my favourite players, the matches I most enjoyed, some funny stories and the joy which was my journey supporting my team for 60 years. I hope you enjoy the rest of my account. It is the musings of an old man trying to remember bygone incidents and trying to honestly admit when these memories are too hazy to be of certain truth. It is peppered with opinions, preferences and prejudices which you may or may not share, but that's fine. The supporters of Wolves are a diverse bunch, but we all live for and support one common cause - the progress and success of our beloved team, Wolverhampton Wanderers.

Chapter 8
Freezing, Baking and Soaking

It's many degrees below zero;
So, don't be a stupid young hero.
Much better you stay close at home today;
I wouldn't watch England in Stone today

OK then, old chap, stay in Stone;
I'll go to the Wolves on my own.
The temperature's lower down there today,
But...I wouldn't watch England in Stone today.

I've waited five weeks, if you please,
No games in this record long freeze.
I'll watch Wolverhampton down there today,
Though too cold to watch England in Stone today.

It's Wolves versus Sheffield U;
There's only one thing I can do.
Though shiv'ring, I'll go to the Wolves today,
It's too cold to watch England in Stone today.

Ten thousand turn up at the ground,
Their minds maybe somewhat unsound!
They've come along eager to see Wolves play,

But... they wouldn't watch England in Stone today.

In the North Bank there isn't a seat,
So, we drum on the floor with our feet.
We need to keep warm any way today;
It's too cold to watch England in Stone today.

The match ends a zero-all draw,
a freezingly apt final score.
Our toes and our fingers fall off today;
It's too cold to watch England in Stone today.

In year 62-63
The great freeze was too much for me,
But I still watched my only team, Wolves, that day;
though too cold to watch England in Stone that day.

In that winter of 1962-63, well remembered as being one of the worst of the 20th century, football fixtures suffered their greatest weather disruption in living memory and no matches were played by Wolves in the five weeks between 16th December and 18th January. They did, in fact, start a match on Boxing day, against West Brom, and were leading 2-0 at half time, but the referee called it off, much to the chagrin of the Wolves supporters, as heavy snow fell before the second-half could start. Albion must have been delighted at getting a second chance but, when the match was restaged in March, they were thrashed 7-0! And so, justice was done.

At last, on 19th January, Wolves found themselves able to put on a match and I was determined to attend, after suffering five weeks of football starvation. No matter that the temperature was still sub-zero - my team was playing a match at home and I was determined to watch it.

We were then living in Stone, some 25 miles north of Wolverhampton, and my means of transport, since I had not yet passed my driving test, was to take the bus to Stafford and then to continue onwards by train to the Mecca of football in the Black Country. I waited that day, shivering and a bit sheepish, at the bus stop in Stone, afraid that any acquaintance of mine would think me bonkers to be going to watch football on such a perishing bitter-cold day. Sure enough, as bad luck would have it, an older work colleague saw me as he drove past on the opposite side of the road. He stopped and wound down his window:

"I take it you're wearing your Wolves scarf to keep yourself warm? Please tell me you're not going to the match."

"Well - er, yes - I thought I'd give it a go," I replied, almost apologetically.

"As I thought!" he exclaimed, metaphorically throwing his hands in the air. "You're stark raving mad. I wouldn't watch England if they were playing in Stone today." And he quickly wound his window back up to keep the warmth in and the weather out and my madness at arm's length.

Well, I can state categorically that I wouldn't have watched England in Stone that day, either, even if they had been playing in my own back garden, but Wolves were a different matter entirely. Given the chance, I would have watched them, whether in Stone or wherever else they might have been playing.

The one memory of the match which, for me, stands out above all others is the incredible sound of feet stamping in unison on the wooden boards of the North Bank floor, like masses of Chinese beating drums together (shades of things to come, maybe?). I can still hear that stamping, which was the only way of maintaining circulation in the toes and lower limbs. I think all the players of Wolves and Sheffield United, the officials and the spectators, including me, deserved medals that day (or else certificates signed by mental health professionals). Despite the valiant best efforts of all the players, they skidded and slithered to a nil-nil draw. Looking back, it is quite surprising that the match was put on at all on such a bitterly cold day. Perhaps the League was growing ever more desperate to attack the backlog of postponed matches. Incidentally, after that freeze-off, there were another four frozen blank weeks before I found myself sitting in the stands at Anfield, to watch us getting well taken apart by Liverpool, 1-4, on another pretty cold day.

Later, when I met and married my wife, she was incredulous that I could watch football in all weathers: "Who would want to sit outside in a cold field in the dark, in the middle of winter and watch a football match?" she wondered. "It isn't in the dark," I protested. "The floodlights are on." I don't think she really understands football.

If that Sheffield match was cold, then August Bank Holiday Monday, 2000, was the complete opposite. My wife and I were spending the weekend down in the southern port town of Portsmouth for an important National Veterans 10k championship race on the road. She was competing in the event, on the outskirts of the town. Coincidentally, Pompey were entertaining Wolves that afternoon at Fratton Park and I didn't wrestle with my conscience for very long before deciding what my right course of action should be in either supporting my loving wife or watching my beloved football team. "After all," I reasoned, "I can't run the race for you. We might as well both make the most productive use of our time."

She said she didn't mind at all and wasn't too grievously hurt and if I preferred to watch the gold shirted outfit kick a ball about instead of shouting her on in an important race then why should she care and "go on then and have a nice time and see you when you decide to come back from the footie and take your time because it's much more productive for you to be at the match and if you don't mind I need to warm up now ". But I suppose I deserved what happened next.

It was a warm day, in fact a blazing hot day, the sun shining out of a cloudless sky. It was a good walk to the ground and I didn't know the way, so I latched on to a crowd wearing blue and white (where had I seen those colours before?). My schoolboy scarf would have come in handy just then, but it had long since been disposed of. I followed in the Pompey fans' footsteps, hiding my (gold) scarf in a bag, just to be on the safe side and trying to look like a local - don't open your mouth, I told myself, for God's sake! Once, when walking to

Stoke City's old ground, I said something to a Stoke fan and he immediately replied with a typical Potteries expression: "You're not from around these parts, are you?" If you want to stay safe, stay dumb!

I began to be aware that the sun was very warm on my head and was beginning to make its presence uncomfortably felt.

I arrived at the ground and found the Wolves end - it was lacking a roof, which was very bad news on such a day. Discomfort grew as the match progressed and I was forced to drape my scarf over my head to protect myself from the searing ultraviolet rays. Of even greater discomfort were the three goals scored by our former striker, Steve Claridge, to set up a handsome 3-1 win for the home side. Wolves' fans not suffering from sunstroke (and those fans who were) slunk off to whence they had come when the match was over - some of them well before the end. I didn't care about anything anymore and walked to the railway station with my scarf protecting my head.

"How was the match?" she asked when I got back with, I thought, a glint of self-satisfied triumphalism in her eyes (I think she had taken pains to find out the result).

"Never mind about that now," I growled. "My head needs some tender loving care."

"How was your race?" I remembered to ask her in the nick of time, amidst my gloom and pain.

In passing, I would remark that the sun can be a problem when sitting in the Steve Bull stand, and many times have its occupants been forced to shield their

I LOVE TO GO A WANDERING

eyes to enable them to watch play on the other side of the pitch. It can particularly be a problem in winter, as the sun sinks low, peeping through the gap between the Sir Jack Hayward Stand and the Billy Wright Stand as it sets.

Aside from being frozen by arctic blasts and baked by tropical suns, the other way in which the elements can attack us on the roofless end of a football ground is by giving us a thorough soaking. And I have certainly been soaked when travelling away, although I can't remember at which ground it occurred. It was either at Crystal Palace's Selhurst Park or at Stoke City's old Victoria Ground. It was probably the latter as I have been to Stoke several times, but only once to Palace. I don't remember the result either, so this hasn't been much of a story at all, has it? I'm sorry about that! The fading memory cells, you know!

In the 60s, I was studying at what was then North Staffs Technical College, later to become North Staffordshire Polytechnic and then Staffordshire University, and I liked to go along to the Victoria Ground to catch a glimpse of Stanley Matthews, George Eastham, Dennis Violett and Alan Hudson. Stoke had a talented forward line in those Tony Waddington days and were good to watch. I enjoyed my visits but must emphasise I never once supported Stoke, not even as a second favourite team. There was only one team for me and I don't think I need to tell you who it was (and still is).

Chapter 9
Peter and Norman

*A finer pair you'll never see
than Peter B and Norman D.
With casual ease P.B. can ping
a ball to Deeley on the wing.*

*But Norman isn't always there;
He roams and wanders everywhere.
If in the box, you're safe to bet
He'll stick the loose ball in the net.*

*Now Stanley Cullis (known as Stan)
is not a compromising man.
He'll haul poor Norman o'er the coals
Each time he misses open goals.*

*But Deeley doesn't really care;
He knows Stan's reasonable and fair.
He's given Norman leave to roam;
Both when away and when at home.*

In an earlier chapter, I nominated Peter Broadbent and Norman Deeley as my all-time favourite players. This is their chapter.

In my opinion, and in the opinions of many, Peter Broadbent was, quite simply, a genius, a wizard on the ball and a total pleasure to watch. It was an absolute privilege to see him play and I'm so lucky to have been around in his heyday. I have seen Stanley Matthews, Tom Finney, Johnny Haynes, George Eastham, Alan Hudson, John White and many other superb ball players in the flesh, but the genius of all of them is topped, in my opinion, by that of Peter Broadbent.

He was the complete player, a magician on the ball, master of the long and short pass and possessing the ability to score a hatful of goals with head or feet. Probably his greatest asset was his devastating body swerve.

One grateful supporter summed it up perfectly when he called out one day from the Waterloo Road Enclosure, as Broadbent weaved his magic on the pitch: "Peter, you're a pleasure to watch." I do hope Peter heard him.

He would sprint down the field with the ball at his feet and the opposition in hot pursuit. Suddenly he would stop dead and trap the ball, sending his opponents careering on past him. Peter had thus made himself the time and space to look up and pick out a pass to his winger, probably Deeley, free on the other side of the pitch.

He could bamboozle defenders with his body swerve; a drop of the shoulder and a twist of his torso and the opponent was thrown off in the wrong direction or left sitting on his backside. I have described how this resulted in a goal at Birmingham's St Andrews in 1958-59.

One day he was leading Tottenham Hotspur a merry dance and Danny Blanchflower, captain of the Londoners, and Northern Ireland's captain too, decided he would have to do something to end the torment. Blanchflower, growing progressively redder in the face at the frustration of it all, launched himself into a full-frontal scything tackle on Peter's feet, which would certainly have resulted in his dismissal today. But it was no sweat for Peter! He opened his legs at the appropriate moment, at the same time moving the ball to the side and out of harm's way with the outside of his left foot. Through the open legs slid Danny, well and truly grounded, and off went our Peter with the ball, and the trademark nonchalant look on his face, as if nothing particularly noteworthy had occurred.

I've already described his superb header against Luton Town, but there was another one he scored which was almost as good (I can't remember the opponents but it was at the South Bank end and I think it was probably against Manchester City). Peter charged down the centre of the pitch as the ball was about to be lofted in from the left. As he reached the edge of the penalty area he launched himself horizontally and met the ball with his head like a rocket. But that wasn't enough for our genius: at the point of contact he arched his neck back slightly and arrowed the ball up into the roof of the net as if it were a guided missile.

Peter Broadbent was in total control of proceedings when he was on the ball. He was like the conductor of an orchestra and everyone danced to his tune and he ran the show. Players were reluctant to tackle him for fear of being made to look foolish.

If I attended a match and found Peter wasn't playing I would feel cheated and short-changed, as you would if you attended the theatre and found the star performer was being understudied that night. Peter was the very best.

Norman Deeley was a small man but he had the rare ability to pop up in front of goal at the right moment and put the ball in the net. If you hadn't been to the match and were looking in the paper next day for the result you would be surprised if Deeley's name wasn't amongst the scorers. He amassed a prodigious number of goals for a winger, but was also a very skilful and brave player. Cullis employed him in the role of a wandering poaching winger, a role in which he excelled, but he could also score from a distance and he headed some good ones as well.

I have described Deeley's outstanding contribution to my first away match at Burnley in 1958. I remember I was watching from the enclosure, a teenage lad with his Wolves scarf firmly wrapped around his neck to keep out the cold fog. Deeley came quite near to me at one point and gave me a quizzical look as if to say: "What's he come all this way for, in the fog, on his own, to watch us get a pummelling? He must be an ardent supporter." At that point in the match it was still nil-nil and we were under aerial bombardment.

Broadbent and Deeley share this chapter because they were the terrible twins, the pair who tormented and terrorised the opposition. They seemed to read each other's minds and were a potent combination. They formed a winning partnership on the right wing and then, later, moved to the left where they were equally as effective. It is worthy of note that, when Deeley left the club in 1962, Broadbent's contribution exhibited a marked decline. They probably both reached a dropping off in their footballing powers at about the same time. Even the genius of a Peter Broadbent eventually, and sadly, comes to an end.

I saw Norman outside the ground on one occasion in the 90s. He was talking to some mates by the Billy Wright statue. As kick-off time approached, he moved off to take up his position in the South Bank, another ex-star and faithful servant not given a seat of honour in the main stand. It was a very sad indictment of the club. I think, at the very least, players who have contributed to winning honours for the club or who have given long and loyal service to Wolverhampton Wanderers, should be given a seat in the main stand free of charge, whenever they wish to attend.

Chapter 10
Away from Home

In my away career, I've done the rounds
of many different clubs and football grounds.

At Fratton Park, the day was very sunny,
But Claridge's three goals weren't very funny.

To see them lose a time or two at Stoke,
In retrospect, is nothing but a joke.

To lose 2-3 at Wigan Athletic
was quite extraordinarily pathetic.

At Coventry, we lost the match to City;
Despite promotion, this was quite a pity.

To win 2-1 at Sheffield United
is quite enough to get the fans excited.

I've visited quite a fair collection of grounds in my following of the Wolves over the years, from Burnley in the north to Portsmouth in the south and from Crystal Palace in the south east to Liverpool in the north west. The clubs I can remember visiting are:

Birmingham City at St Andrew's;
Bolton Wanderers at the Reebok Stadium;

Burnley at Turf Moor;
Coventry City at Highfield Road;
Crystal Palace at Selhurst Park;
Derby County at the Baseball Ground;
Fulham at Craven Cottage;
Hednesford Town at Keys Park;
Huddersfield Town at the McAlpine Stadium;
Liverpool at Anfield;
MK DONS at Stadium MK;
Oldham Athletic at Boundary Park;
Portsmouth at Fratton Park;
Preston North End at Deepdale;
QPR at Loftus Road;
Rotherham United at the New York Stadium;
Sheffield United at Bramall Lane;
Stoke City at the Victoria Ground;
Tottenham Hotspur at White Hart Lane;
West Bromwich Albion at the Hawthorns;
Wigan Athletic at the DW Stadium;

And two special ones:
Cardiff - Millennium Stadium and
Wembley Stadium - the Twin Towers.

Certainly, I have visited all the grounds mentioned, some of them more than once, and possibly a few more grounds than these, but I can no longer remember the results of all the matches I attended, or even when they were. I feel that we lost more than we won when I travelled but there were some good results which stand out in my memory, and I will describe some of these in this chapter.

I set off on a very adventurous journey with my brother for an FA Cup third round tie in January 1967. I had by then been a qualified driver for just under a year and I directed the car over the Peaks in the middle of winter, through Leek, Buxton, Chapel-en-le-Frith and Glossop to Oldham, where we took on the Athletic at Boundary Park. Things didn't go too well for us at all for the first 88 minutes and we found ourselves 0-2 down with two minutes left to play, and on our way out of the cup to lower-league opposition.

A rare goal from cultured fullback Bobby Thomson gave some respectability to the score in the last two minutes. It seemed to be too little much too late but then, to our amazement and delight, skipper Mike Bailey forced the ball home, just beating the referee, who had his whistle in his mouth, and blew it immediately after the goal was scored. The hearts of the locals, who thought they had secured a famous victory against their 1st Division opponents, were broken but the joy of us Wolves fans knew no bounds - the ones still in the ground, that is. It was a happy drive back over the high moors in the dark and we did them over comprehensively in the replay.

The story goes that a generous and ecstatic Oldham supporter left the ground a few minutes early so that he could line up celebratory drinks for all his mates down the working men's club. I'm not sure if many of his mates showed up for their free pints in the end, and he probably drowned his sorrows by quaffing most of them himself. The ground, in fact, was quite empty before the finish, the more disgruntled Wolves fans having given up at two goals down. When we met some of them outside the ground after the match and remarked on how well we had done to save the match, they thought we were being sarcastic!

Another great away day memory I cherish is of the match in which Terry Wharton scored a fabulous goal against Sheffield United at Bramall Lane in 1962-63. Wolves won that match by two goals to one and it was the third of the club's record five successive away victories with which they started that campaign so well. I remember the goal for two main reasons: firstly, it was probably the hardest shot I have ever seen and secondly, it was so simple and unvarnished in its execution - just two players involved, one pass and one shot, and covering almost the full length and width of the pitch.

Alan Hinton picked up a loose ball on the left side of the pitch, just level with his own penalty area, and advanced down the flank towards the halfway line. Before he got there, he looked up and spotted his fellow winger hugging the right-hand touchline, way over in the distance on the opposite side of the pitch. Hinton hit an amazing cross field pass - all of 50 metres - which landed just in front of Wharton who, without taking a touch, drew back his right foot and hammered the ball into the far top corner of the net from his position almost on the touchline. The shot was so hard it nearly uprooted the goal posts. I heard a home fan comment at half time: "That winger of theirs can shoot a bit!"

The "10k to MK" initiative was a fabulous day out, towards the end of Kenny Jackett's promotion-winning season from the third tier of English football in 2013-14. The gold and black hordes completely took over one end of the ground and were in right good voice throughout the afternoon. It was a tight match and it was not until the later stages that Liam McAlinden rose to be the first to get his head to a free kick and score a wonderful winner which took us inexorably on towards promotion. McAlinden never really made the grade at Wolves, but he certainly produced the goods that day.

The whole afternoon was conducted in a spirit of camaraderie and sportsmanship and the home club are to be congratulated for hosting such a friendly and trouble-free event.

I took my younger daughter to a couple of away matches around the turn of the century and we travelled by coach to both games. The first one was a happy and friendly affair, but the second turned a bit ugly at the end.

My daughter was 12 years of age when we arrived by coach in good time at Queen's Park Rangers, in 1999, giving us the opportunity to spend lunch time in the pub and meet several people from a Wolves emailing list I contributed to in those days and which was one of the forerunners of the Molineux Mix internet forum, of which I am a member today.

After a pleasant and sociable lunch, we walked to the compact Loftus Road ground where we found ourselves housed in the lower tier behind one goal.

This was somewhat claustrophobic and of restricted vision but, nevertheless, it afforded us an excellent view of the only goal of the game being headed in down our end, late in the game, by Steve Sedgley, the controversial transfer swap from Ipswich Town, with Mark Venus going the other way. Manager Colin Lee and his assistant, John Ward, went ape on the touchline when the header went in.

Earlier, my 12-year-old daughter had been the centre of attention in the refreshment area at half-time, where her Bully hat, horns and all, was admired by the fascinated locals.

The second trip I took her on was an evening excursion by coach to our nearest foes, West Bromwich Albion, in 2001. We were escorted to the ground by the police and escorted back again after the match. Little trouble occurred. On the pitch Nathan Blake gave us the lead but we had to settle for a 1-1 draw in the end. If my memory serves me correctly, there was some controversy about the harshness of the free kick decision that led to the Albion equaliser.

Back on the road, our coach was circling the large roundabout, prior to heading north up the M5, when a tremendous THWACK resonated by my head. A bystander, or should I say a thug, noting the loyalties of the coach and its occupants, decided to hurl a brick at my head. It was a considerable shock to me and my daughter but, thankfully, the window stood firm.

There were a few disappointments along the way when visiting away grounds. A massive crowd overfilled Coventry's Highfield Road ground for the 2nd Division

Championship decider in 1967 but the Sky Blues were too good for us on the day, as George Curtis and his hard men muscled out Dougan, Knowles and co. Curtis was a very tough cookie, the hard nut who all opposing fans loved to hate. But we finished 2nd and were promoted back to the top division at the second time of asking, so all was well enough.

Nor was the farewell to the Premier League in 2012 any more enthralling. This was a farewell in a downwards direction, as we celebrated (?) our first of two successive relegations. We started brightly enough, Matt Jarvis giving us the lead, but then it was a typical capitulation as we ended up vanquished 2-3. After the match, we waited for the players outside the ground. Jarvis was very civil, but cagey, when I asked him if he would be remaining for next season's Championship campaign: "We'll see," was all he would reveal.

Last season a carload of us travelled to Preston on the day of the notorious Steve Morgan car park contretemps, when he was assailed by fans, unhappy with the way things were going and with the toothless performance they had just witnessed. We were unaware of the incident until the next day, but there was a dark mood on the terraces as the match progressed. When it came time to descend from the heights of the Deepdale stand my Parkinson's caused me to freeze and I had to be supported down by my Steve Bull Stand buddies - more about them later.

You may be wondering why Hednesford Town's ground is included in a list of stadia visited to watch Wolves. This occasion was a fitness trial for Steve Bull in a match for Wolves' third team (one below the reserves). It was in the 90s sometime and I think a young lad named Jones scored a hat-trick. I remember Mark Atkins playing in the match and I was impressed by his professionalism as he stuck to his task at a competitive level well below his talents. It made a refreshing change to get right back to the grass roots of football at this friendly ground, and I think it demonstrated how my daughter and I would go virtually anywhere to see Stevie Bull.

As football grounds go, undoubtedly the muddiest and most grassless of them all was Derby County's old Baseball Ground. Molineux could be a bit sticky at times (see my description of the cup tie against Bolton Wanderers in 1959) but Derby's ground was in a class of its own, a veritable gluepot of a pitch. I remember watching a good Wolves win there, but can't remember when. I think the score may have been 3-0 to the good guys.

Of course, the best away days were the visits to Wembley and Cardiff in 1974 and 2003. I'll have more to say about these in the next chapter.

Chapter 11
Wembley and Cardiff

Dave's done it, and the Wolves are back.
A grateful thumbs-up from Sir Jack.

Remember back in '74
Wolves triumphed - they could give no more.

From the second and the third millennium,
Two great Wolves teams - so thanks a million.

Manchester City were rated red hot favourites by the bookies and most of the pundits to win the 1974 League Cup final at Wembley, and small wonder, when you consider they could parade a forward line as talented as Mike Summerbee, Colin Bell, Francis Lee, Dennis Law and Rodney Marsh. Mind you, their Wolves counterparts of Kenny Hibbitt, Alan Sunderland, John Richards, Derek Dougan and David Wagtaffe were no slouches either. Whatever the bookies' odds might have been, we set off on coaches from Wolverhampton on 2nd March 1974, full of hope, and confident our boys would not let us down. They didn't.

There was a cross-country athletics race scheduled for that same day, but there was absolutely no way I was going to miss this Wembley occasion for my running, even though it was the National Cross-Country Championships, the biggest date on the domestic cross-country calendar. I gave my team my managerial apologies, instructed my stand-in on what needed to be done and headed down south with my brother.

There was quite an armada (if that is the right collective term) of coaches, heading down the M6 and M1 motorways from the two cities of Manchester and Wolverhampton, and rival coachloads taunted each other in friendly fashion as they trailed their scarves out of the windows in a stream of colour. No trouble occurred at the motorway service stations - all fans were focused on the match ahead and harboured no thoughts of senseless violence. Wolves were quietly confident, while City couldn't see any way they could lose the match.

There was something magical and symbolic as we approached the twin towers at the far end of Wembley Way. Just as Hindus make pilgrimage to the Taj Mahal, Moslems celebrate their Hajj at Mecca, Catholics gather at St Peter's Basilica in Rome, and tourists and monarchists peer through the railings of Buckingham Palace, so football fans long for the day when they have the right to surge up Wembley Way as one of two sets of supporters whose teams are competing for a major prize on the hallowed pitch that day. Wembley is the spiritual home of football in England and it is every fan's dream to be there supporting their team. I missed out in 1960 and had to watch them win the FA Cup Final on the telly, but in 1974 I was there to savour the moment to the full.

We Wolves fans were on the terracing behind the goal that Wolves were defending in the first half and we saw at first hand the string of fine saves young Gary Pierce pulled off to defy the rampaging City. He continued to keep us in the game after the interval, with a quite magnificent performance on his 23rd birthday. I reckon he must have made at least 23 saves, one for each year of his life; It was his only game of the eight which the team played in the competition that season and he earned his medal as much as anybody.

There were other golden-shirted heroes on the pitch that day. Kenny Hibbitt sent us into delirium with a trademark volley which put us in the lead just before half-time, but it wasn't long into the second-half before Dennis Law breached Pierce's defences at last, and we feared the worst. Manchester City streamed forward with wave upon wave of attack, but we held firm, inspired by skipper Mike Bailey who drove us on in typically swashbuckling style. Dave Wagstaffe was limping on the left wing and had to be replaced by Barry Powell. John Richards was also struggling, with an injured pelvis, but he disguised it well and battled on. And in the last ten minutes, I think it was, King John magnificently slammed the ball home for his eighth goal in the competition, and Wolves had won the cup!

It was pandemonium on the terraces as we bounced up and down, hugged total strangers and shed tears of joy and relief. It was a release of all the pent-up emotion we had bottled since the last trophy win of 14 years previously. Yes, just 14 short years had elapsed since the FA Cup victory but it seemed like a lifetime. In those 14 years, we had gone from being a team at the very peak of the game down to a finishing position of 6th in the 2nd Division, before clawing our way back into the top flight. And now we had won a trophy again. No matter that it was the relatively minor competition of the League Cup - to us at the time it was a major win and we savoured it to the full.

The play-off final at Cardiff's Millennium Stadium in season 2002-03, which saw us reach the Premier League for the first time, was another magical occasion. With the renaming of the league divisions this match was classified as the Division 1 play-off final although it was, in effect, the 2nd division of English football from which we and Sheffield United were battling to escape.

The match took place on the Spring Bank Holiday Monday, and it was an early start for me and my younger daughter to catch the special train laid on for our journey to the Millennium Stadium. Wembley was being reconstructed and was unavailable but the trip to Cardiff still seemed like a pilgrimage to the Mecca of, if not English then British, football.

The Wolves throng seemed to take over the centre of Cardiff, as the fans drank and partied on the streets - and this was before the match! The great Sir Jack Hayward, for whom this was a very special day, appeared on the streets and blessed the crowd. Eventually it was time that we took up our seats in the magnificent stadium, high in the upper tiers. The gold and black colours seemed to dwarf the red and white of Sheffield; would the team do likewise on the pitch?

We had been too long in the 2nd tier of English football. Since Graham Turner masterminded our elevation to that level in 1988-89 we had remained there, with no play-off final appearances. There had, however, been two heartbreak semi-final play-offs in which we had lost to Bolton Wanderers (controversially) and to Crystal Palace. This time we had beaten Reading in the semis and today was to be our day of destiny.

The first half was just a blur of incredulous ecstasy, as goals from Mark Kennedy, Nathan Blake and Kenny Miller swept us into an unassailable 3-0 half-time lead. Down in the bar at half-time there was raucous celebration, as fans tried to come to terms with what they had just witnessed. The stewards looked shell-shocked at this outpouring of emotion and bedlam.

Despite the score, we were all nervous wrecks for most of the 2nd half, realising that one goal for the Blades could change everything. Matt Murray made himself the hero of the day when he saved a penalty to deny the Blades that goal we had feared and, as the match moved into its last 15 minutes, we at last began to believe that it was ours and that promotion was assured. Sir Jack's famous thumbs up appeared on the big screen and all was safe. Dave Jones had repaid the faith shown in him by Sir Jack by managing the team to glorious promotion.

Celebrations were unbounded and, well after the presentation had come to an end, a sea of gold scarves rippled and waved from one half of the ground, while the other half was empty. Empty, that is, all but for a solitary Yorkshire couple, sitting hand in hand, sad and lonely, high in the arena, watching the unbridled joy which was not in their own hearts. I thought it was noble and generous of them to stay behind, happy for us but with regretful thoughts of what might have been for them. That is what football should be all about.

Eventually the celebrations had to end and we trooped off to the station to catch the train home. We encountered the Sheffield faithful, travelling part of the way on the same train as us, who seemed remarkably cheerful, given the circumstances. We, on the other hand, were celebrated-out and must have looked somewhat down and anticlimactic.

"What's the matter with you lot?" enquired one puzzled Tyke. "You've just won promotion and yet you look even more miserable than we feel."

"I think we're worrying about next season," I ventured, by way of an explanation.

How prophetic would that worry turn out to be! By the end of the following season we were back in the 2nd Division.

Chapter 12
Glory Hunters

True fans support through thick and thin,
But glory hunters only in
the good times, not the bad.

We lose, and take it on the chin;
They lose, and simply pack it in;
allegiance just a fad.

We'll still support, lose draw or win
But 'lose' and 'draw' are just not in
Their dictionary - that's sad.

We're proper fans; we'll keep supporting
the Wolves. They spend their time reporting
Each new allegiance - mad!

Is it a possibility I could be accused of being a glory hunter? After all, I grew up in the leafy, rural Home Counties and yet ended up supporting Wolves from the industrial Midlands, who were then the top team in the land. When I moved home to live close to them Wolves were about to win their first Championship and were revered by an adoring TV audience as vanquishers of Europe - and I jumped on that band-waggon, an outsider supporting a team almost from another world.

And so, I am an obvious glory hunter - guilty as charged.

But hold on a bit; did I have any choice in the matter? There were no football league teams close to where I lived in Berkshire. Headington United, later to metamorphose into Oxford United, were not then in the league, and neither were Wycombe Wanderers. Milton Keynes Dons had not yet been conceived, nor even had Milton Keynes itself. So, there were no local league teams to support, unless you count Reading, which was a lot further away.

So, you will agree that when I started school in Wolverhampton, by then living seven miles away from the Black Country town, it was right and proper that I should support Wolves, by then my most local team (I break out in a sweat when I think how that original blue and white scarf might have led me down another road, too dark to contemplate). So, now supporting my local team, I am exonerated and found not guilty of the capital charge of glory hunting.

Glory hunters - don't you just despise them! They swan around and preen themselves in the reflected glory of whoever happens to be the flavour of the moment. Who hasn't seen the platforms of Wolverhampton or Stafford railway stations, festooned with the red or blue colours of hordes of football supporters, off up north to Liverpool or Manchester, or down south to Chelsea or Arsenal? Or maybe you have seen claret and blues or (heaven defend us) blue and white stripes off to the Second City and its surrounds, when they could just as easily have stayed in their home town to watch their soccer - very misguided and perverse of them indeed.

How good it would be if our young school boys and girls pledged their allegiance to their local team, instead of looking further afield and supporting some big club, just because their favourite celebrity is one of its fans. What a boost that would be to the local club's coffers if they did give their local team their support, making the club less reliant on the largesse of some rich or profit-seeking benefactor and levelling the playing field so that the small-town club could more easily compete with the large city side. This could spell the death knell to the obscenely large TV contracts and player's salaries in force today and lead to the possibility once again, of any club from anywhere having at least some hope of winning the top honours.

Wolves, in fact, punched well above their weight in the 50s, being as they were an industrial town club taking on, and beating, the metropolitan and big city giants. But they had a large and enthusiastic local following which was keen to support their local team, and they regularly attracted 50,000+ crowds. Spurs sought to end Wolves' dominance with big-money spending on stars such as Dave Mackay, Alan Gilzean and Martin Chivers, while Wolves were happy to develop their own local talent. One must admit, though, that in addition to recruiting from local talent, Wolves also ran a thriving nursery team at Wath in Yorkshire, from whence came the two greats, Ron Flowers and Roy Swinbourne, amongst others.

My wife, though not really understanding football, has some wise words to say at times. "How can a grown man be as totally wedded to a particular football team as you are to Wolves?" she will ask me. I explain that it is deeply ingrained in one's DNA, buried deep within the genes, a local and a tribal loyalty that cannot be resisted. "But how can you say you support Wolverhampton when half your players may come from up north somewhere, or from Ireland, some more might hail from London or East Anglia and the rest perhaps from Spain or Africa or Portugal. And how can a Chelsea fan revere Fred Bloggs one day and then revile him the next, after he's been transferred to Liverpool?"

As I say, she doesn't really understand football. Everybody knows that Chelsea would never have a player by the name of Fred Bloggs on their books - nor, even, would Liverpool, come to that!

Is it possible to have a second favourite team? I think it is. We all have transitory second teams every time we watch a match on the telly and find ourselves rooting for one team or the other. But our loyalties only last for the duration of the match. How many people jumped on the Leicester City band-waggon in 2015-16, when they pulled off that spectacular and unlikely Premier League title win against the rich big boys? How many of those "supporters" can no longer give a fig for Leicester, now that they have returned to their rightful level? Glory hunters, the lot of them!

Mind you, there's a case to be made for every school child having a second team, holding loyalties to their local amateur side, as well as to their closest professional league team. They could support them on alternate weekends, pocket money allowing, and thus prime the grass roots of football with much needed funding.

So, do we think glory hunters are misguided and unpleasant people? I need to be careful what I say here! I've mentioned my two nephews who slid down the slippery slope and took up support of two unmentionable north-western teams. They were brought up in Newport, very close to Wolverhampton, in the 70s but must have come under the pressure of the times at school. Their younger brother, however, latched on to his local team in the dark days of the 80s and has remained steadfast ever since - one of the best! Mind you, he does have a second team - living near MK and being unable to travel he holds an affection for the Dons but, on the day of the 10k to MK game, there was no doubt as to where his primary loyalties lay, and he cheered as loudly as any when McAlinden's header went in the net.

If the truth were known, I have some pretty shady characters in my family, as far as football is concerned. My good wife was born in Liverpool but her family moved to Codsall, where her brother was born, and then to Stafford. He started off supporting Wolves and even had the kit, I believe. Then, just because his cousins and uncles all lived on Merseyside, he switched allegiance to the Reds. Switched allegiance from the one and only Wolves! He must be the only person in history to have done such a thing. No wonder I am so gleeful whenever Liverpool lose.

Having said that, my two friends, who have recently been driving me to the matches, both attended the great Cup win at Anfield this season (2016-17) and they have nothing but praise for the Liverpool supporters. They found them to be cheerful and friendly, gracious in defeat, happy for us and said how well we had played; and they mixed amicably with the Wolves supporters in city-centre pubs after the match. Let's just put my antagonism down to friendly family rivalry, and nothing more. We are all football supporters, when all is said and done, and all have our own loves and loyalties.

I have some trouble in my family regarding football, what with having Spurs and Liverpool and Manchester United supporters in their number! But I and my siblings, my children and one of my nephews have kept the faith - Wolves forever, ay we! We could never imagine ourselves being anything else.

Chapter 13
Them Lot down the Road

The Wolves are our beloved side;
We wear their colours with great pride.
But let me mention right-away
We dislike W. B. A.

About promotion we can dream
For England's greatest football team;
But please believe me when I say
That we don't fancy West B. A.

Near Sandwell Valley's where they're from;
that team of stripy shirts, West Brom.
But it's quite clear that, come what may,
We do not like West Bromwich A.

Our Molineux's a house of gold;
The Hawthorns leaves us feeling cold.
What follows may cause pandemonium:
We just don't love West Bromwich Albion.

Now, before we get on to 'them lot' down the road, let's clear something up - have you ever wanted Wolves to lose a game? If you have then you must hate some other team more than you love Wolves and that means you are not a true supporter. Shame on you! That's my view, and I hold to it with conviction.

Consider this hypothetical situation: Wolves hate team A with great passion, for various reasons we don't need to go into. It is the last weekend of the season, and both team A and team B are in dire danger of relegation. If team B win then team A will go down; any other result and team B will be for the chop. Wolves are playing team B! What do you want the result to be?

There's a seeming dilemma here. We would absolutely love it - LOVE IT - if team A went down, but that will only happen if we lose to team B. Any other result and they will stay up. By winning our last match, against Team B we will save A's bacon. Now, a true Wolves supporter would bury their prejudices, accept the disappointment and take the points by winning their match against B, even though it saves team A's skin. Jubilant supporters of Team A would then flood the Wolves message boards, thanking supporters for saving their status by beating their rivals. The irony is that quite possibly, the next season, team A could screw Wolves up by, say, putting a spanner in their promotion prospects. But that's how loyalty pans out in this funny old game of football. No true supporter can wish their team to lose in any match.

It always strikes me as twisted logic to extol the virtues of Wolves but then denigrate all other teams. If all teams, bar one, are rubbish then where is the credit in beating them? On the contrary, there must be a serious malfunction if we fail to beat them. How can the greatest team in the world fail to beat a rubbish team like Chelsea, for instance? No, we should admire Chelsea and the rest of the top teams and admit that, although Wolves are the love of our life, they are not the greatest team in the world any more. And, whisper it, West Bromwich aren't all that bad! Well, not completely. And whisper it again - I don't hate West Bromwich Albion, nor do I hate Leeds United, nor Liverpool, nor even Tottenham Hotspur. There, that's done it. Nobody's going to read the rest of the book now, and I had some more interesting things to say. Editor, can you stick this chapter at the end of the book, please, or cut it out altogether!

The above is logical enough but football isn't about logic. It's about passion and tribalism and emotion and love and hate. When the stripy team come to the Custard Bowl or we go to the Poorthorns we hate each other with a vengeance, and the chants and insults come thick and fast. Some of the singing, regrettably, is not for a family audience, but these are ancient enemies, fighting out ancient battles which will never be resolved. What was Moxey thinking of, giving over the South Bank to the Stripes that time? How did we cope with the 1-5 mauling which spelt the end of Mick McCarthy? Did Albion weep in their beer when we beat them 7-0 in the great-freeze season of 1962-63? What about 1954 for them or the choke season for us? (that was season 2001-2002 when we squandered an 11-points lead over the Baggies, and their storming finish saw them go up instead of us). The pendulum swings back and forth and a Black Country derby is a cauldron of bitter atmosphere but tinged on both sides, I would suggest, with a touch of respect for the other side.

And when it's all over it is back to normal life, with one set of fans basking in the bragging rights, unless it's a draw of course. Rival fans might be workmates next day or members of the same family home. They are human beings, men and women, just as we are; neighbours and friends, husbands and wives. Until the next derby, that is, when another passionate tribal battle will be fought on the field to the death.

Wolverhampton Wanderers v West Bromwich Albion is the greatest derby match in the world (and, to boot, probably the one with the most letters in its description).

Some supporters get their minds addled, and confuse raw football tribalism with real life. The feuds, the hatred and the partisanship reside on the field of play and in the factories and offices where merciless bragging rights are taken up. They do not and cannot exist outside the game itself. Sometimes this cut-off point between pitch and outside world becomes a bit blurred and extends from the turnstile, which should be the boundary, to the surrounding streets and the wider world. That is why sometimes visiting supporters are herded like cattle to and from the ground by local police.

But there should be no need for this humiliating shepherding. Football rivalry and true hatred have no place beyond the amphitheatre in which the battle takes place. I have absolutely no truck whatsoever with football violence and hooliganism, inside or outside the stadium. If that brick hurled at our coach as we returned from the derby at the Hawthorns had penetrated the glass then I wouldn't be here now, penning these opinions and reminiscences; far worse, I could have lost my beloved daughter.

It sickens me to the pit of my stomach to hear supporters from any club boast that they gave Chelsea, or Leeds, or Birmingham or whoever a good hiding. That's not what football is about, and such violence has no place in the beautiful game.

All true football supporters are passionate people, loving their clubs as we love Wolves. They have a right to walk this earth, following their team and unmolested by intimidation and violence. All right, we know they are misguided - Wolves is the only club to love and support - but they have the right to make their choice and to live in peace.

Right, pompous pontificating over and we move on to the next chapter.

Chapter 14
Let's Have a Sing-Song

The Molineux Roar came well before
The North Bank choir, then really quite dire.

But news got around by word of mouth,
And repartee blossomed from North and South.

It wasn't until quite a few years later
That friendly Jez Moxey banned the Liquidator.

How strange he should do so, we must say,
The song simply asked them to "please go away."

I've already remarked that some memories are still fresh in my mind, but that others have lost themselves in the mists of time. Memory is a funny old thing. I bet Ron Flowers and Gerry Harris, the only two players still living who played in the first match I attended, in November 1957, can't remember many, if any, incidents from that game - they are older than me, so perhaps I should remember a little bit more than they do. But what I quote as memories I can still recall. This chapter is a random collection of this and that, of things that come to mind as I think of days long gone. But, as its title suggests, it's mainly about choirs and chants and roars.

Back in the 50s there was not the same organised singing at grounds as there is today. Nowadays the South Bank will go through a whole repertoire of songs, before and during the match - tribal songs, humorous, mocking and near the knuckle songs. Back in the 50s there was little or no chanting, but I remember one day when Everton came to town.

I was on the South Bank under the roof and there was quite a crowd of their supporters further down in the uncovered section, chanting away - I can't remember what they were singing but it would probably have been about the virtues of their favourites from Merseyside (and probably something derogatory about another team from the banks of that same river). Anyway, they were proving to be somewhat of an annoyance, and I wished they would desist. Surely, they couldn't keep it up for the duration of the match? Perhaps a Wolves goal or two would shut them up. What did shut them up was the Molineux Roar.

The Molineux Roar was something else and, sadly, is not heard today. It was a deep-throated AAAAAARRRRRRHHHHHH sound, issuing from thousands of larynxes simultaneously and reverberating around the ground in a cacophony of noise. It had no accompanying words - it was just a mighty roar. The Scots talk about the Hampden Park Roar, but I can't see how it could have been greater than its Molineux counterpart. Our roar was resonant and throbbing and it was just awesome to be part of it and engulfed by it. Nothing I have heard since comes anywhere close to it. It was the reason why teams were terrified to visit

Molineux - if the Wolves play didn't batter them down, then the ROAR would.

It shut the Everton singers up that day. Once the match started the roar commenced and their chants and songs were totally obliterated and we didn't hear a peep out of them for the rest of the match. They probably continued chanting, but no one could hear them anymore. What the score was, I have no idea, nor when the match was played, but vivid in my memory is the sound of that roar on the day when we silenced the Everton singers.

Mind you, we did have a rudimentary "choir" back in those distant days. When I went to Burnley for my first away match in 1958 I tagged on to a group of about 50 Wolves supporters walking from the station and followed them to the ground. They had a leader who conducted proceedings and, when he started, the others would follow:

"Zigger-zagger, zigger-zagger, WANDERERS; zigger-zagger, zigger-zagger, WANDERERS. One-two-three-four listen to the Molineux roar. Five-six-seven-eight who do we appreciate? W.O.L.V.E.S. WWWOOOLLLVVVEEESSS!" This they repeated ad nauseam through the very centre of the town, to the great annoyance and alarm of the local Saturday shoppers, while I, an embarrassed school boy wearing gold, walked by with my head down and pretended I wasn't with them.

As an aside, this reminds me of an incident on the big anti-war rally in 2003 when a million or more of us marched through the streets of London to express our opposition to the pending Iraq war. A section of the crowd had their own zigger-zagger man, who intoned:

"One-two-three four" to which the marchers replied: "We don't want this bloody war."

Zigger-zagger man: "Five-six-seven-eight."

Marchers (paraphrased): "Think again - it's not too late."

Well, this went on for a good while until zigger-zagger man was almost completely hoarse. He handed over to his sidekick while he recovered his voice.

Sidekick: "One-two-three-four"

Marchers: "We don't want this bloody war."

Sidekick: <a pregnant and extended pause> "Help! I can't remember what comes next," he pleaded, desperately.

"Five-six-seven-eight?" suggested zigger-zagger man, helpfully, if a little hoarsely.

All those within earshot dissolved in convulsive mirth.

It was probably in the late 60s or early 70s when stadia football choirs took off in a big way. Ours was housed, surprisingly enough, in the smaller North Bank end, but the low roof made the atmosphere in that end feel raucous and exciting to a person (me) in his late twenties. Then the South Bank set up in opposition and there was repartee and banter between the two ends: "Peter Knowles - Burnside". "Peter Knowles - Burnside" reverberated back and forth, extolling the virtues of the two contenders for the playmaker role at that time. It was entertaining stuff but, sadly, it replaced the Molineux Roar which has gone, probably never to return. Nowadays, the North Bank seems staid in comparison with the South, only a notch or two up in exuberance from the Billy Wright Stand. So, moving round the stands in an anti-clockwise direction (looking down from above) the noise levels decline from the Sir jack Hayward Stand (the South Bank), via the Steve Bull and the Stan Cullis (the North Bank) to the Billy Wright - the quietest stand of all.

People in the Billy Wright seem to be less demonstrative than elsewhere in the ground. Perhaps they come predominantly from the older generation of Wolves fans, brought up in more sober days, when people didn't wear their hearts on their sleeves quite as much as they do today. Certainly, there were not the histrionics on the pitch that we see today, where players roll over ten times, hoping to con the referee into awarding a penalty or sending off an opponent. And there were no shirts-off, leaping-into-the-crowd goal celebrations either. I remember a particularly fine goal scored by Jimmy Murray, after which he politely shook the hand of his nearest teammate before trotting back to his position. He would be buried under a mass of colleagues if he scored such a goal today.

Perhaps having literally to bear the weight of most of the team on top of them every time they score a goal is one reason why strikers seem to be injured so often today. In that case, our current set of strikers should be relatively injury free, the cynic might say.

The old Molineux Roar lent a unique atmosphere to the ground, which the current South Bank choir does too, but in a slightly less intense way. Maybe they will be the loudest in history if the corners are ever filled in to retain the atmosphere.

Another noise familiar in the old days was the sound of the ubiquitous wooden rattle, which made a harsh, clattering noise. I never possessed one myself but they appeared to require much wrist action to operate them. It was quite a sight in the ground, seeing a phalanx of rattles being enthusiastically - er - rattled when a goal was scored. Eventually they were banned, presumably for health and safety reasons, and are another item consigned to the annals of football history.

But to get back to the atmosphere in stadia. A certain night-time match produced an atmosphere in Molineux that exceeded any ever known in the great stadium, topping even the Molineux Roar days. That match was the play-off semi-final 2nd leg match against Crystal Palace in 1996-97, and it will be the subject of its own chapter.

Does anything about football irritate you? I'll tell you what annoys me intensely and that is the style of speaking by football commentators and reporters. You'll hear Jeff Stelling announce "Wolves have just scored at Molineux and we'll go there now to hear about it. Over to you, Bianca Westwood."

Now the events that Bianca was about to describe were as follows: Jordan Graham ran down the left wing, beat three defenders and delivered a high cross which the goalie dropped at the feet of Nouha Dicko, who blasted it into the net. How Bianca described it was: "Graham weaves his magic down the left flank; he takes out three defenders and crosses a high ball. The goalie half-catches the ball, juggles with it, and then drops it at the feet of the grateful Dicko, who blasts it home. It's one nil to Wolves, Jeff."

You see what's happening? The goal has already been scored before we even hear from the reporter at the match. The reporter describes it in the present tense, as if the action was taking place as she speaks. Why can't they talk about what has already occurred, in the past tense? That's my gripe - not very important, I know, but annoying to me.

I'm also niggled when people (newspaper reporters and editors mostly) describe football teams as "outfits". All right, I know I did, a few chapters back, but that was intentional, so that I could develop the point here. Outfits are the clothes people wear, not a cherished team that fans go bananas over when they score a goal. "The Molineux outfit is preparing for the cup tie on Saturday." I hope the outfit keeps its owner warm - what nonsense!

Another thing I really do not like is the intermittent international breaks we are forced to endure several times each season. They disrupt the flow of club football and leave us without a match for two whole weeks. I'm not a great patriot and much prefer anything Wolves to anything England (see chapter eight, where I describe going to Molineux on a bitter day in 1963 but declare I wouldn't have watched England in my own back garden on that same day). I realise the need for these international get-togethers but they are damned annoying all the same.

Back in the old days Wolves had to carry on and play their matches without Wright, and sometimes without other players as well, when international matches cropped up. If you were good enough to have international players in your team then you were good enough to manage without them for a match or two.

The close season in the summer is also hard to get through, and I try to absorb myself in cricket and tennis to while away the months. I enjoy rooting for the England cricket team more than I do for our footballers. This must be because the only football team that really matters to me is my beloved Wolves. And long gone are the days when the England team was chock-full of Wolves players. There is such a preponderance of London-based players in the England squad that it is little surprise so many younger players of good pedigree gravitate to the Metropolis.

Steve Bull was a good enough striker to play for and score for England while, at the same time, playing for a club which, at the time of his first cap, had just been promoted from the third level of English football. Such a selection would be undreamt of by today's selectors.

Chapter 15
Need'st Thou Run
So Many Miles About?
(William Shakespeare's Richard III)

Why do you run so very many miles around?
It's better if you take your normal seat within the ground.
Sit with your friends and mates, enjoy the game and watch
The constant to-and-fro unfold - much better at the match.

Not more about running! What's that got to do with football, with being a Wolves supporter? Well, running is an essential thread, woven throughout this book, and is an important essence of my life and being. If I was you and reading this book I might turn to the next chapter, or I might throw the book away, or - possibly - read on and see what the connection is. OK, just in case you are carrying on reading, I will carry on writing and tell you how my running has been interwoven with my football over a lifetime. But if you don't read this chapter you won't hear about my best mate, Kim.

Sometimes, my love for running has been so strong that I have missed a match at Molineux. On other occasions, the siren call of Molineux has been so irresistible that I have skipped an important race and handed over my duties to somebody else, before disappearing down to the Mol. On 2nd March 1974 that's exactly what I did, except that, on that occasion, I disappeared down Wembley Way instead.

The two pulls of football and running often tear me apart and leave me with great feelings of guilt. Am I a true Wolves supporter? How can I be, when I don't attend all the matches and am lured away by something that must be more important to me than football is? I contend, however, that I am a true supporter, that the thought of Wolves consumes me constantly and that I can think of nothing else on match day but what the latest score might be. I even think of them during the actual running of a tough race, when my lungs are bursting and my legs are screaming for me to stop. When I do finally finish, my first action (after bending over and getting my breath back) is to try to find out the result or the latest score.

Taking a celebrity at random: Richard Osman, of "Pointless" fame, claims to be an avid Fulham supporter, and I've no doubt he is. But I bet, with his busy lifestyle, he doesn't get to all the matches. His career comes first. Likewise, so did my athletics career. I was paid nothing for it; in fact, I shelled out a whole fistful of notes in pursuance of it, but it was still a career, albeit an amateur one. Incidentally, Osman was most gracious when we beat his favourites at the Cottage this season, and he remarked how he couldn't understand how we could be 16th in the league. As we see them more often than he does, we can understand it much better than he can!

I don't claim to be a great supporter, but I am a devoted one, although not as devoted as some. There are fans who travel hundreds of miles each week, both home and away, in following their beloved team, and I am not fit to lace their boots. There are different degrees of support and these special fans should be made life members of the club, with special privileges granted to them. I suppose my only claim to fame is that I have been supporting the Wolves for a long time. But even then, there are people who have been attending for far longer than I have - a gentleman who sits near me in the Steve Bull stand tells me he has been coming down to the ground for 70 years! We each need to live with our own consciences in the matter, and not denigrate anyone else's attendance record, or puff ourselves up undeservedly over our own.

In my running career, I have competed in one thousand two hundred and thirty-two races, over distances ranging from 100 metres to the full marathon (26.2 miles) and, in the process, have covered sixty-six thousand, five hundred and seventy-nine miles. That's a fair distance to drive in a car and illustrates my commitment to my athletics career. How do I know these figures are true?

Well, I have kept paper records, and every time I have run a race I have written down the details and updated my race total by one. When training or racing I have similarly updated the total mileage by the amount I have just run. This is, of necessity, approximate, as I cannot know precisely how far I have run, if I go out for a spin on Cannock Chase, for example. But a runner knows his or her body - he knows how long he has been out and how he has felt in the session and how fast he has been running. And I have been careful to underestimate my daily mileage, so as not to overestimate the total career mileage covered. And so, I am confident in saying I have run at least 66,579 miles in my lifetime.

Do I record each football match I have attended? Sadly, no, and it is a source of deep regret that I haven't done so. Perhaps even more memories would have stirred in my brain if I had a written record to refer to. All those old 6d programmes, edited by the one and only Ivan Sharpe, the "Pink" newspaper cuttings written by the peerless Phil Morgan - all lost in house moves, or thrown out in spring cleaning purges; Wolves nostalgia lost forever. Undoubtedly, I was a more enthusiastic running historian than I was a Wolves one. And yet I have never written a book about my running, but here I am writing from memory about my life-long love affair with Wolves. That must say something about how much I care for my football team.

Where did I practice all my running miles? I ran on the Downsbanks and the Common Plot in Stone, on Tittensor Chase and in Hanchurch Woods and, most of all, on my beloved Cannock Chase. I had a little black mongrel dog, a faithful running companion, and it was his beloved Cannock Chase too. To respect their privacy, I have not, so far, named anyone in this book - but I know that Kim won't mind if you know his name.

He lived for 17 years and adored accompanying me on 20-mile training runs on Sundays. It's more likely he ran closer to 30 miles as he deviated off into the forest, returning a few minutes later, barking and deliriously happy. He would get back home from the Chase, devour his meal and then flop down in front of a blazing fire (if it was winter) and sleep out the day. He was my faithful training companion, my light and my joy.

It was harrowing to see him decline in his old age. He still ached to come with me but could, by then, run barely half a mile. I took to running around the playing fields of Shugborough Estate, so that he could lie in the middle, watch me gyrating round the perimeter and sniff around a bit.

In the hot June of 1986 his dear and loving heart was failing. In the middle of the night he stood in our room, gasping for breath, and we knew the time had come. I lifted him in my arms and carried him to the car. Even then he was excited, thinking we were going for a run on the Chase. I felt like a total betrayer as I drove him to his destiny. He gave me total loyalty and unconditional love but I was perpetrating this shameful deed upon him.

On the vet's table tears soaked my beard as the needle was pushed home. The vet withdrew discreetly and I was left alone with the lifeless Kim, cradling my friend and loving soulmate in my arms. After a decent interval had elapsed, the vet returned: "That will be £15 please."

Some weeks earlier I had asked a Chase Ranger friend of mine if I could bury my dog on the Chase when he died. "Sorry, I'm a bit deaf - I didn't hear that," was his apologetic reply. When I got back from the vet's surgery on that gruesome night, now lightening into dawn, I carried Kim onto the Chase in a blanket, with a large spade in my other hand. Who should drive by but my friend, the Chase ranger? I do hope he paid better attention to his driving when he got out on to the open road, as he didn't seem to see me at all - something on the other side of the track appeared to take up the whole of his attention.

Kim rests peacefully, where bluebells bloom in May, at one with the ground he loved so much.

The writing of this chapter has affected me more than I can express in words, and so I will leave the subject of running for a later chapter and return now to matters pertaining to Wolves.

Chapter 16
Some Matches
You Never Forget

Sometimes you'll find a scoreless draw
Is nothing but a total bore.
But if both teams get three or four,
Then that provides a thrilling score.

But if in most games you get beat,
That's not a very happy treat.
You probably will carp and bleat,
If your opponents dive and cheat.

But if your man's hit on the shin
And, fast-reacting, knocks it in,
The crowd will make a frightful din;
for nothing pleases like a win.

I've mentioned some great matches I have really enjoyed, and some that I haven't. Here are a few more, in both categories.

Before any professional match today, both teams will come out onto the pitch, 30 minutes or more before kick-off, and practice elaborate warm-up drills, before leaving the pitch for last-minute preparations, before they re-emerge, just before the start. Back in the old days, no such pre-match practice took place out on the pitch. The teams ran out, the captains shook hands and tossed up, and the match was underway. What routines they practised in the changing rooms before emerging on to the pitch remain veiled in mystery. I think the present-day practice detracts from the magic of long ago, when our favourites appeared to a fanfare, just before the match started, and we rose to acclaim them (that was when we heard the "Happy Wanderer" played). Today, we've already had half an hour of them before they leave the pitch and then come back on again. It detracts from the impact somewhat. Perhaps that's why fans don't take up their seats until a few minutes before kick-off.

On 22nd October 1960, Sheffield Wednesday decided to anticipate the modern trend by coming out on to the pitch a good 10 minutes before the start time and kicking about with gusto and going through all sorts of drills, obviously hoping to catch Wolves cold and unprepared. Wolves duly emerged from the dressing rooms with barely two minutes to spare, kicked off and were three goals to the good within the first 10 minutes. So much for going through a thorough warm-up routine! The final score was 4-1, and I don't suppose Wednesday tried those tactics again in a hurry.

Incidentally, I don't think there were so many injuries, back in the 60s, so how useful or sensible are these pre-match drills? It's worthy of note that we have had two goalkeepers injured in the pre-match warm ups within weeks of one another this season. Any athlete will tell you the importance of pre-event stretching to render muscles and ligaments supple, but I wonder if we take it a little bit too far these days.

Another quick-fire opening occurred when Newcastle United were our visitors on 31st October 1959. Wolves came out, kicked off and within two minutes were 2-0 up. We licked our lips, expecting an avalanche of goals, but 2-0 was the way it stayed. Newcastle, perhaps fearful of our goal-scoring reputation, must have adopted a damage limitation strategy with 88 minutes still to play in the match!

One of the most enjoyable matches for me occurred on 27th November 1965, when, once again, it was the hapless Pompey who leaked a bucketful of goals; perhaps it was punishment for that wretched bell ringer of theirs who assailed our ears every time we played their team (I think the annoying sound was known as the "Pompey Bells"). John Holsgrove (2), Hughie McIlmoyle (2), Bobby Woodruff (2), Ron Flowers and David Wagstaffe did the plundering, and the half time score was an amazing 6-0. Down in the bar at half-time everybody was laughing - there was little else you could do. I don't suppose the Pompey supporters found much to laugh about, however. The second half was a bit of an anti-climax, as so often seems to be the case. We were sufficiently into winter for there to be a second half blizzard, which tore into the faces of the Wolves players. We did manage to score twice more, but so did Portsmouth, and the final score was 8-2, one of the rare occasions when a double-figure aggregate of goals has been scored in a match involving us.

We might have laughed over that match, and we certainly did over another one, on 3rd November 1971, a UEFA Cup tie against Den Haag of Holland. I was mentoring a university student at work - he was undertaking his year of industrial experience. He was a Burnley supporter for his sins but enjoyed trips to Molineux with me to see the antics of Dougan, McCalliog, Richards and Bailey. So, we went along to the evening Den Haag match. What was the feature of this match which caused us such hilarity?

The source of amusement, in fact, was a hat-trick, the funniest one we had ever seen. You might well ask the question: how is it possible for a hat-trick to be funny? They are usually a delight or a tragedy, according to which side you are on. But this was a hat-trick scored by three different players, three players from the same side, a hat-trick of own goals! The Den Haag players were so terrified of Derek Dougan that they strained every sinew in their bodies to keep Wagstaffe's crosses from reaching him. They succeeded, but only by diverting three of the said crosses into their own net. We were rolling around, splitting our sides. Every time Wagstaffe crossed the ball from the left, it seemed a Dutch player got a toe on it, taking it away from Dougan and at the same time beating his own goalie. It really was incredibly amusing, for all but the unfortunate Dutch players.

After the match, we dashed back to my friend's halls of residence to watch it all again on Match of the Day, treating ourselves to another dose of side-splitting laughter at Holland's expense, this time with the assistance of some liquid refreshment.

I was present for Derek Dougan's Molineux debut on 25th March 1967, and what a virtuoso one-man show it was. Dougan had made a quiet debut the previous week in a 1-0 win at Plymouth (in which he didn't score) and he was very much on trial in this, his second match for the club, in front of the Molineux crowd. The great man endeared himself to the crowd by scoring a hat-trick, but the goal that really sealed it for his relationship with the fans was the hat-trick goal itself. The ball was played into the big man, who had his back to goal. The said big man, still on crowd probation, flicked the ball over his own head, turned on the spot and lashed the dropping ball into the net on the volley. I was in the North Bank and remember every magic moment of it. The crowd erupted and he was our hero from that moment onwards.

Oh, and by the way - we were playing Hull City, the final score was 4-0 and Peter Knowles weighed in with the other goal. I thought I would just mention that, although only one thing really mattered that day.

There are many, many more great wins to remember, but too many to describe here: Mick McCarthy's promotion winning match back to the Premier League in 2009, Kenny Jackett's promotion straight back from League One at the first attempt, aided by that amazing 6-4 thriller against Rotherham United, and the great turnaround against Birmingham City at Molineux when Andy Thompson equalised with a late penalty and then

Steve Bull swept home Simon Osborn's sublime ball over the top to break Birmingham hearts. Bull was a little bit naughty after the goal, wheeling away from the North Bank and gloating in front of the Brummie contingent in the Steve Bull lower, but emotion took hold of him, as it did everyone else of a Wolves persuasion.

But, having told you of some of my great memories of famous wins, here's one from the opposite end of the spectrum, and I certainly didn't enjoy it at all. In 1968 Wolves had a rising young star on their books, by the name of Alun Evans, and Liverpool took a shine to him. He was duly transferred to them for a large sum of money and, a week later, came back to play against us at Molineux. The bare statistics of the match are sufficient comment: Wolves 0 Liverpool 6, with Evans scoring two goals. A Liverpool supporter goaded me - "not a bad player, is he?" and "he looks better in red, don't you think?" If I remember correctly, Evans didn't have much of a career with Liverpool, but he certainly humiliated us that day.

Chapter 17
That Atmospheric Night

That night the tension was insane;
It won't be quite like that again.
We sought to reach the heights sublime;
We were convinced it was our time.

That sound assailed both mind and ear,
that sonic, crushing atmosphere.
A wonder Palace stayed that night;
It would have made the brave take flight.

Three Palace goals at Selhurst Park
plunged Wolverhampton into dark.
We tried to pull it back, but failed;
Promotion once again de-railed.

The night of 14th May 1997, was an occasion never to be forgotten by anyone who was there. The atmosphere was electric, in fact it was cosmic, no - it was stratospheric, or even galactic. This was the Division One play-off semi-final, 2nd leg, and the crowd was there to suck their team into the play-off final for the Premier League for the first time in their history. If an intimidating atmosphere could have done it alone, then Wolves would have been one match away from promotion without even kicking a ball that night.

Mind you, the first leg the week before in south east London hadn't gone very well at all. The match was beamed back to Wolverhampton and I watched it from the Billy Wright stand. Quite a large crowd assembled, and we went through the whole gamut of emotions. We cheered when Jamie Smith, our marauding young wing back who later joined Palace, scored, we groaned when Palace got a goal and we buried our heads in our hands when Dougie Freedman, later to become our striker, scored a late, late goal to set up a comfortable 3-1 first leg lead for the Londoners. But we weren't despairing; nor were we down and out - we had an away goal under our belts and we felt that, if we could manage an early goal in the second leg, we could pull it off. A two-nil score line would be required to secure the win in normal time.

Tickets for the match were very hard to come by, but I managed to purchase two, high up in the wings of the Billy Wright Stand, almost equivalent to sitting in the South Bank. My 10-year-old daughter was with me and we settled into our seats in trepidation. It was the 28th anniversary of my father's death and I was sure he would be setting his Tottenham allegiances to one side for once so that he could be with us on this special night.

You could cut the atmosphere with a knife as you entered the arena, and that, indeed, was what it was - an ancient gladiatorial amphitheatre, where two teams would fight head to head and toe to toe to the death, where the gods would raise their thumbs to acclaim one team and lower them to damn the other. We were in the Colosseum of ancient Rome, and there could only be one winner.

Crystal Palace must have wondered what had hit them as they entered that furnace, that cauldron of emotion and baying sound (Steve Coppell, their manager, later said it was the most intimidating atmosphere he had ever encountered). Wave upon wave of cacophonic bedlam descended on them from every point in the ground. Each stand gave of its utmost and, for one night in its lifetime, the Billy Wright was up there with the best. The great fighter himself, a Wolves man through and through, was conducting his own stand from above. Divine intervention was raining down on us that night.

The tension was unbearable as we willed the fruits of that super galactic atmosphere to shine down on our team. We knew we had to score early and hit them when they were down. We couldn't allow them to reap any inspiration from the atmosphere themselves. But Palace held firm and the tension and the anxiety grew more and more intense.

And then Mark Atkins scored. The stadium exploded. Now we just needed one more goal and we would be through, if Palace didn't score an away goal. But shock and disaster - Palace did score, not only an away goal, but an equaliser on the night. We were back to square one, but it was worse than that, because the away goal meant that we needed to score three more times if we were to go through in 90 minutes, avoiding extra time. David Hopkin, the ginger haired bane of our lives at that time, was the player who equalised, to appal the crowd and to temporarily turn the atmosphere down a notch or two. Now we needed two more goals again, just to force extra time. But the atmosphere soon ratchetted itself back up to manic levels again.

Would you believe it, even in that furnace of passion, there was one moaner, the solitary whingeing sniper in the whole stadium, and he was sitting a few seats adjacent to mine. "You've only yourself to blame," he bawled at Atkins for a misplaced pass which caused a promising move to break down; he castigated Mike Stowell for a poor kick; he had a go at Bully for not finding the net. But he was the only one - the rest of the crowd, to a man, woman and child, drove the team on.

And then I did something I never do, on that of all nights. I left early. My daughter needed to be up for school the next morning and I needed to beat the traffic away so that I could get her into bed by 10 o'clock. There was not much time left and hopes were fading but, as we walked north up Waterloo Road, still feeling the crazy atmosphere, even outside the ground, a thunderous roar told us that Wolves had scored again. It was now 2-1 (we later discovered it was Adie Williams who had got the goal) and we were now just one goal behind, but that was the way it stayed. As we hurried back to our car, parked in a residential area just off the Stafford Road, we strained our ears but could hear no further roars. The gods on high, who had been concentrating all their energies on Molineux that night, to the exclusion of exploding galaxies, crushing black holes and the almighty storm in Jupiter's Great

Red Spot, finally lost interest in football and turned their attentions back to Jupiter.

We had been similarly disappointed a few years before, in 1994-95, when we lost to Bolton in controversial circumstances. A 2-1 victory at Molineux had been followed by a 0-2 defeat at Burnden Park where, it was alleged, a certain Bolton player had felled David Kelly with a punch, delivered conveniently behind the referee's back. Lots of conspiracy theories abound - but we don't want to be branded as whingeing losers. Suffice to say, it was hard to take and Steve Bull lay on the pitch at the end of the match, heartbroken that possibly his last chance of top-grade football had slipped through his grasp.

It would be another six years after Crystal Palace before we had our next attempt at reaching the play-off final, but - WHAT A NIGHT that was against the Palace!

Chapter 18
My Family
and Lots of Animals

I've told you all about my little dog,
but not about our self-adopted mog.

Abandoned, lost, it wandered all alone,
And then decided ours would be its home.

It climbed up on the kitchen windowsill,
Fussed round, meowed, ate, drank and had its fill

Stay then, so long as you've got no bad habits,
Unlike our former house-trained, fighting rabbits,

Or our two lovebirds - one just had to go;
The poor cock was attacked and lost his toe

So - creatures great and small, as you can see.
We had a very large menagerie.

But there's a group round which my life revolves;
A pack of hunting, fighting, hungry WOLVES!

My running continued after Kim. It's true, I no longer had to wait for him, or run round in circles so that he could sit in the middle, safe in the knowledge that I wasn't far away, but that wasn't the point - I wanted him to be there, I wanted to have to wait for him, and my runs on the Chase were sad pilgrimages for many years, as I toiled along in memory of and in honour of his doggie love, often visiting his grave, deep in the forest where I had lain him to rest.

We had plenty of four-footed friends after that, but no dogs or cats - well, a cat did make its home with us at a much later date, but I'll come to that. And there were quite a few creatures of the two-legged, feathered variety as well.

Whilst the children were little we generally had a pair of budgerigars and a pair of gerbils, both at the same time. The gerbils lived for no more than two years, and it was noticeable that, when one died, the other would follow it to the Heavenly treadmill within a day or two. There were many funeral services and animal burials in our back garden.

The budgies lived much longer, if we could keep them from flying away, that is. They had the freedom of our lounge during the day, to fly around to their hearts' content but, sadly, a few escaped through carelessly left-open windows and doors. When I was a child we had a budgie that could recite "Hey diddle-diddle" all the way through and word perfectly. Also, at the same time, we had a cat named Sandy and the budgie addressed him as "Sandy, the pussy", as we had taught him to do. One day, the budgie displayed his intelligence and verbal skills by extracting a word from the nursery rhyme and addressing the feline as "Sandy, the CAT"!

One day a woman picked me up in her car to take me to a meeting and as we drove away I pointed to our front window. "Do you see my birds in the window?" I queried. "Oh yes, very colourful," she replied, giving me a rather strange look, I thought. Anyway, by the end of the day we returned from the meeting and, as she drew up outside the house, she remarked, just to make polite conversation: "I see your birds are no longer in the window." "Oh no," I replied, "They will have flown down the other end long ago. They much prefer it down there, where they can see into the garden, rather than on the front window, watching the traffic go past." A look of embarrassment and relief coloured her face: "I'm so sorry. I thought they were ornaments."

She must have taken me for a right wally for keeping, as she thought, a pair of rather dubious bird-like ornaments on display in the window and showing them off to visitors!

Our budgies did not enjoy an entirely harmonious friendship with the gerbils. We had often seen them flutter outside the gerbils' cage and taunt the little rodents and, one day, we returned home to find blood on the birds' feathers and on the bars of the gerbils' cage, so there must have been a bit of a skirmish while we were out, with the gerbils fighting back against the birds' aerial assaults.

One day a gentleman found an escaped and lost lovebird in our street and he knocked on our door because he knew we kept birds. We housed the bird for a few days until we found out who her owners were and could reunite her with them. However, we were careful not to let her fly at the same time as our budgies, in case something untoward occurred. Despite this, our male budgie took a real shine to this female lovebird, although confined within his cage, and was severely reprimanded by our hen budgie for letting his wandering eyes get the better of him.

There was a rota at our kids' school for bringing the class hamster home on Fridays so that it didn't starve to death over the weekend, and our turn to care for it came around. Now I'm a less than able handyman but was very proud of the boxing-in job I had performed on a rather unsightly central heating pipe in the lounge. But the hamster went missing and, after much frantic searching, we could hear it scrabbling about inside this box. There was nothing for it but to tear apart my pride and joy to rescue the little rodent; the alternative of a starved or baked hamster to report to school on Monday morning was too horrible to contemplate.

After we had finished with budgies and gerbils in our home our 16-year-old daughter acquired a leopard gecko and, when she went off to university, dumped it on us to take care of for the rest of its 10 years or so of life. It was a charming creature, but not very cuddly as it spent a large proportion of its time in a heated tank, where it fed on live crickets (dead ones it was not interested in). It seemed to have a remarkable ability to escape from its tank, leaving no trace of how it had got out. One morning I came down to discover it was missing and, after much searching around, I found it snuggled under a low but large settee. I lifted the corner of the heavy piece of furniture a fraction while my younger daughter picked Gizmo out. I told her to be quick about it, or I would be forced to drop the heavy item on the poor lizard. She, the lizard, was icy cold after spending the night out of her heated tank.

There are lots more menagerie-based stories I wanted to tell you - about two house rabbits who fought tooth and nail; the giant New Zealand white would thunder down the lounge (like Steve Kindon), heading directly for its little black housemate, who would flatten itself to the carpet at the very last minute as the giant shot by above it; about two lovebirds who were anything but loving (the hen bit the cock's toe off) and about the cat that adopted itself into the family, to the peril of the birds - but you don't want to hear them. For the love of god, get back to football, you say. So, still in mourning for my dog Kim, I will get back to football. But I will mention one more animal type, if I may be so bold, with which I have some affinity - and that is a pack of magnificent Molineux WOLVES, mentioned in the sub-title of this book.

Chapter 19
Lost in the Mists of Time

*It's hard to keep a match day log
when all the ground's obscured by fog.*

*You can't maintain a scorers' list
when teams are hidden in the mist.*

*The ref should call an end to it
and replay when the weather's fit.*

Many of our memories are lost in the mists of time. Our recollection of past events is often foggy and distorted. As we grow older our memory deteriorates and images fade away into vagueness. Clarity is conspicuous by its absence. But what if the event we are trying to recall is itself intrinsically unclear and literally shrouded in fog? Such an event occurred many years ago when Wolves took on Everton (we seem to have a lot of memorable happenings when Everton travel down to play us).

Visibility was extremely poor from the start of the match, and from my "vantage" point on the South Bank I couldn't see much of the ground beyond the halfway line. Sound was muffled by the thick mist and I could only assume that Wolves failed to score down the other end - Everton certainly didn't score in the South Bank goal; that much I could see. The players somehow groped their way off for the half-time break and we waited to see if visibility would improve for the second half. It didn't.

At the start of the second half the mist, which had thickened into a peasouper of a fog, was so dense that the halfway line was no longer visible; in fact, we couldn't see much beyond the penalty area. Muffled sounds, cheers perhaps, could be faintly heard from the far end of the ground (not goal celebrations for Everton, we hoped) and then suddenly a Wolves player would appear in the South Bank penalty area, to be repelled by the Everton defence, which was obliged to react quickly to the sudden appearance of a golden-shirted apparition, materialising out of the murk.

Time went by and we judged that full-time must be coming up at any moment. All we could see was the Everton goalie in his area, peering intently into the fog, hoping an opponent wouldn't suddenly materialise in front of him. As it turned out, he had been guarding his goal for five minutes after the referee had blown for time and the other 21 players had trooped off the pitch. When he was eventually missed in the changing room a colleague was sent out on a mission to locate him in the fog and rescue him from his devotion far beyond the call of duty.

It transpired that Everton had won the match 3-0, although you could have told us any score and we would have been obliged to believe it. How the referee didn't see fit to call off the match remains a mystery to this day. He shouldn't have even started it. It is the only match I have ever attended where I witnessed less than 50% of the play (and that includes the Spurs match of 1960 when I didn't get onto the terraces until half time and saw nothing of the first half). By rights, the whole crowd should have received a refund.

On another occasion, in very murky conditions, I was walking to the ground to see Wolves play Blackpool but, as I approached the Molineux Hotel, the crowd all seemed to be moving in the opposite direction. "It's been called off, mate. "The ref thinks it's too foggy." It was very disappointing, but much better than having another experience like the Everton match.

Under conditions like those I have just described, the Everton match would never have taken place today. It's quite interesting to consider other ways in which the match day experience differs between now and in days gone by.

Today, so long as you have purchased a ticket, you are guaranteed a seat, whether you are a season ticket holder or not. Provided you have a ticket you will have exclusive use of the corresponding seat. But back in the days of yore a standing place on the terraces had to be found for all but the privileged few (those who could afford a season ticket in the stands). The crowd would arrive early and for a big match, with 50,000+ spectators crammed into Molineux, the ground would be full a good hour before the start. Today, seats are taken up five minutes or less before kick-off. It makes it very hard to estimate how many are in attendance that day. Back in the day, I loved to stand on the North Bank and watch the South Bank fill up with the pinkish colour of people's faces. If the terracing was full, there were 30,000 people in; if the horizontal gangways filled up, then there were 35 to 40k inside the ground and if all the vertical and horizontal gangways were crammed, then the crowd was 50k plus.

The players ran out to the strains of the "Happy Wanderer" - 'I love to go a wandering along the mountain track...', et cetera. Today, it is Elgar's Pomp and Circumstance march and "Hi Ho Silver Lining" (but certainly not the Liquidator - Chief Executive, Jez Moxey, banned it on the advice of the Police because some of the words were a little bit rude and inflammatory).

Today, opposing fans hurl abuse and taunts at each other. But back then, it was the Molineux Roar which took the place of chants and singing. Half-time lasted just 10 minutes and it was rare if the Saturday afternoon match was not over by 4.45pm. Almost invariably, Saturday matches kicked off at 3pm, with midweek matches starting at 7.30pm on Wednesdays. Sunday matches were unheard of and, I believe, not permitted by law at that time.

Most people stayed in their places at half-time, so I can only assume that not much drinking was undertaken. Toilets are not much less primitive now than they were then - they were disgraceful, pretty much, then and they are now, if you ask me. But then, it must be quite hard to cater for 50,000 bladders in a comparatively confined area. The toilet experience is degrading, to put it mildly. Having said that, the best toilets we ever saw were at the DW Stadium in Wigan. They were quite palatial, compared to those in other grounds, including ours.

A man was employed to manually hang out the half time scores on a long, horizontal board, at the North Bank end of the Molineux Street Enclosure, whilst another man did similarly at the South Bank end of the Waterloo Road Enclosure. It was as if they were hanging out the washing to dry. I bet it raised gasps at other grounds when 6-0 went up on their boards the day Wolves beat Portsmouth 8-2. I never saw the final scores go up - perhaps I left too promptly. Today, we have announcements and TV monitors to inform us of what is happening or has happened elsewhere.

I don't remember how effective the PA system was, back in the 50s, but today it is nothing short of diabolical. This is one area of the Molineux match day experience which requires urgent attention.

Today, the hard-core supporters in the Sir Jack Hayward Stand are on their feet for most of the game, but each is in his or her own place and can rest their bum on the back of the seat if they get tired. Back in the 50s you were either rammed against a crush barrier or held up by the pressure of bodies around you. I have literally been supported by my shoulders, with feet off the ground for the entire match.

My sister and I were once at Villa Park for a cup semi-final (not involving Wolves), in a crushing mass of humanity. We started off side by side and, as the afternoon progressed, we orbited one another like a planet circling the sun, first she above me, and I to her left, then she below me and I to her right - and so on.

We managed to reunite with each other at the end of the match!

We were following Swansea Town (now City) in their great cup run, in solidarity with a friend from Wales whom we had met on holiday - not supporting them, you understand, but rooting for them nonetheless, against their higher-league opponents. They were sadly beaten by Preston North End in that semi-final, in which a teenage Howard Kendall played for Preston. Swansea had a marvellous win against Liverpool at Anfield in the quarter-finals and I remember we travelled to the ground on the bus from Lime Street station. One cocky Liverpool supporter could hardly contain himself at the prospect of a big win: "Well, at least Everton have the consolation that they can't lose today," he crowed (Everton had been knocked out in an earlier round). Liverpool had no such consolation, sadly for him.

Incidentally, I remember going to Villa Park for that semi-final ticketless, and being lucky enough to purchase two tickets from a kind gentleman outside the ground for face value - my first (and only) dealing with ticket touts.

Probably the most comfortable place to be situated on the old terraces was just in front of a crush barrier but, when a goal was scored, everyone fell downwards by about 10 steps. It is amazing that more catastrophes didn't occur, and it took the Hillsborough tragedy to put an end to such insane herding of humanity, and the tragic fire at Bradford to force clubs, ours included, to demolish and replace rotting and unsafe stadia.

It's easy to be unduly nostalgic for the things of days gone by, but I really found the four floodlight pylons at each corner of the ground evocative. They could be seen from a distance away, and the light they shed raised excitement and expectation of the action to come as one approached the ground from across town.

In conclusion, the nineteen fifties and the twenty tens were very different experiences, neither one better nor worse than the other - just somewhat different experiences. But they always involved our beloved team, Wolves.

Chapter 20
Attendance Record

To Molineux I've come, both man and boy,
for 60 seasons' worth of pain and joy.
I hope I've been an ardent, loyal fan
from back in 57, when I began.

So much has changed since that far-distant day,
but not my eagerness to see Wolves play.
Through all the days of hardship, toil and strife,
to watch them's been a huge part of my life.

As of May 2017, it is fifty-nine and a half years since I first attended a match at Molineux but that doesn't mean that I have been a constant attender over all those decades. I certainly saw most of the latter part of the 50s, from 1957 onwards, the 60s and a good chunk of the 70s, but my 80s' attendance was very poor. I came back in the 90s with my daughter, to enjoy the later Bully years and then, in the first decade of the new century, I purchased my first ever season ticket. Finally, in the 2010s, my attendance is falling away again and, on 7th May 2017, I will be hanging up my hat and scarf and, like the Duke of Edinburgh, will be retiring from active engagements.

Whether my rather sketchy attendance record described above makes me a good supporter or not, the club has seen fit to honour me with a special send off on 7th May, and I am honoured to accept their kindness and generosity, but I accept it on behalf of all supporters, most of them better than me, who are the lifeblood of the club and are its future. I thank them, and I also thank Wolves. I am overwhelmed by all the kindness shown.

I saw out the Cullis era, and was there through the Andy Beattie, Ronnie Allen and Bill McGarry years, but I missed most of the other managers' regimes until coming back to regular attendance in the Graham Taylor years. There were several reasons why my attendance was so sparse during the late 70s and through the 80s. One big factor was the violence which took hold of the game, both on the streets and in the stadia. It was a blot on our great game - the beautiful game - and I wanted no part of it. I supported the team but not some of the so-called supporters, who shamed our great club, and brought disrepute to football in general. The violence led to segregation of rival fans who, in my early days, had mingled happily on the terraces together. Football was shamed and I stayed away from it.

Also, around this time, I changed my job and was sent by my department to retrain as a computer programmer in London. This gave me the opportunity to see Wolves when they came to London (I remember visiting Crystal Palace and Tottenham Hotspur), but it made home attendance difficult. When I first started work in London I drove down to the capital early on Monday morning, returning on Friday evening - no, don't even think about it! Friday evenings on the M1 were horrendous, even in the 1980s.

While I was away in London during the week, Kim would pine for me. But, come Friday, my mum, whom I lived with at the time, would tell him I was coming home that day and he would spend the rest of Friday on the back of the sofa, looking out of the window until I made an appearance. He was ecstatic when he saw me arrive. It was very humbling to be so adored and trusted by another being. But later, I was to betray that trust.

After about a year my London bed-sit became unavailable and I decided not to search for another lonely, grotty room to spend the week in but, instead, to commute to London and back each day.

It was some commute. I would rise at 5am, leave home at 5.45am to drive to Wolverhampton railway station, get the 6.30am train to Euston, arriving there at 8.30am, sprint for the tube to London Bridge, where I would catch another train to Plumstead, to arrive at work for 9.30am. A truncated lunch break permitted me to leave for home at 4.30pm, reversing the morning journey to arrive back home in Stone for 8.15pm, a total travelling time of seven and a half hours each day.

I didn't go straight home but changed into my running kit in the car and did a 30 minutes training run before entering the house. This was to avoid upsetting Kim, who would have been distraught if I had come home and gone straight out again without him. When I did finally enter the house, his joy was unbounded. There was just time for tea, before falling into bed for six hours sleep and then rising to do it all again next day. Weekends were bliss, but there was little energy left for going to football.

I did this horrendous commute for a year, before finding a job close to home. Every day there were the same faces on the train, tired and drawn, and for all I know, the owners of those faces carried on with their commute long after I stopped, even up to their retirement, possibly. It was no way to live.

Later, in the 80s, I married and had a family and this became another bar to my attending matches. I couldn't swan off to Molineux and leave my wife to change the nappies and bring up the children on her own. I went back to Wolves when my daughters were old enough to accompany me.

And it was my younger daughter who accompanied me to matches in her primary school days, in the 90s, when Bully was supreme. She absolutely loved him and wore her Bully hat with great pride wherever she went. I've described our trips to QPR and WBA and there was another, notorious, occasion we were together when I met an old schoolmate in Wolverhampton. He was the very same person who had 'outed' me as a Wolves supporter in 1957, when he saw me buying a programme before the Burnley match. Anyway, on this occasion, he was over for a holiday in the UK, having become domiciled as a citizen of Australia, and we had agreed to meet in a Wolverhampton pub.

We entered the hostelry and I made happy reunion with my old classmate, but it wasn't long before a member of staff came towards us menacingly. He wondered if I was aware that children were not welcome in his friendly inn and could I please see my way to leaving the establishment and taking my daughter with me - IF I would be so kind. My daughter and I had, essentially, been thrown out of a town centre pub. Later, as we sat in the Billy Wright Stand, waiting for the match to start, a loud Aussie accent wafted down from above - "FOOTBALL HOOLIGANS!"

I have been called that on one other occasion. I was availing myself of the toilet facilities at a running event and had trouble flushing the said contraption. I removed the cistern lid to adjust the ballcock and then replaced the lid, to the accompaniment of much banging and clanging. A voice issued from outside the cubicle: "I know what you're up to in there, vandalising the toilets, Lawrence -bloody football hooligan!"

My love for the club never waned during the several years I failed to visit the football ground. On a match-day I could think of nothing else but the upcoming Wolves match and I counted down the hours remaining to kick-off time. I catch up on the score in various ways when I am not at the game. I have an alert on my mobile phone which tells me when a goal is scored in a match involving my beloved team. This system doesn't always work as desired, the alerts sometimes coming in several hours or even days late. When the phone does beep a shiver goes down my spine and I daren't look at the screen immediately in case it is bad news.

By far the best way to keep up with the action is to watch Jeff Stelling on Sky Sports on Saturday afternoons. Instant updates are given and Stelling's presentation, statistical knowledge and quick brain are a delight. Next best is the Commentary thread on Molineux Mix, which gives the score in real time, together with a lively debate on how Wolves are performing (that's once you have got past 30 or 40 posts of "YEEEESSSS", "Get in", "GOAL!", "You Beauty", and other rapturous comments - but since these mean Wolves have scored, who's complaining?).

I remember following on TV the progress of the West Ham v Wolves match from Upton Park on 23rd March 2010 - I think it was being shown live, although I can't be certain whether I was just watching the score updates or not. Anyway, the score was 1-0 to Wolves for some time. I left the room momentarily for a natural break and when I returned just a few minutes later I did a double take when I saw the score had changed, rapidly and most agreeably to 3-0. The match finished 3-1 in our favour.

Incidentally, this game was the third of a remarkable trio of matches in a period of a week, in which we beat Burnley 2-1, followed by a 2-2 draw with Villa and then the West Ham match, all of them away from home. Why were these three matches so remarkable? Was it because they were all away from home? No, nothing very strange about that - three away matches in a row were by no means unheard of. Why, then? Were the grounds very close together? No - one was in the north, one in the Midlands and one in London. What was so unique about them, then? Do you give up? I'll tell you - Burnley, Aston Villa and West Ham United all play in claret and blue; they may be the only three teams in the league who wear those colours (no, I've just looked it up and find that Scunthorpe United also wear claret and blue) and we played them in three successive away matches in the Premier League and took seven points off them out of nine available. I find it fascinating and a bizarre coincidence, anyway, even if it fazes you not!

Getting results when away on holiday abroad can be a nightmare. Sometimes, it is necessary to wait for the English newspaper the following day, and then the result isn't always in it. Bars are invariably showing the wrong channels and tourists you speak to haven't heard of Wolves or they have no interest in the result; "But I know how Chelsea got on if you're interested, mate." I've taken to ringing my sister and, in the middle of telling her about our holiday, just casually dropping it into the conversation - "oh, by the way, do you happen to know how Wolves got on today?" - trying to make the question not seem like the main purpose of the phone call! If I don't find out Wolves' score I am frantic and can't relax.

I even nip out of wedding receptions to sneak to the car and switch on the sports service on the radio or slip away from parties for, ostensibly, an extended toilet break. There is no limit to the lengths a hard-core supporter like me will go to find out the score. Waiting is not an option - I need to know and I need to know NOW.

Now that my Molineux career is coming to an end I will be sitting down in front of Jeff Stelling every Saturday to hear his words frighten me: "The deadlock has been broken at Molineux - but which way has it gone?" He is a tease!

Chapter 21
Season Ticket Holder

I cannot think of any earthly reason
Why not to buy a ticket for the season.

Once you have paid the cash out, it all ends
in days of entertainment with your friends.

In rain or shine, no matter what the weather,
You will, at Wolves, enjoy the match together.

When I was diagnosed with Parkinson's in 2007 and was forced to give up running I decided that I wouldn't let the condition rule my life; I would carry on with all the activities I normally did for as long as I could do them. And one of those activities was going to watch the Wolves at Molineux. To avoid the hassle of queueing at the ticket office on the day or booking online, I would take out my first-ever season ticket and watch the matches regularly from the Steve Bull Stand. How I came to choose J8 Row B Seat 201 in season 2007-08 I have no idea, but I'm so glad I did because I couldn't have chosen to be surrounded by a nicer bunch of people. I'm going to miss them so much when I leave Molineux at the end of this season. I hope all other season ticket holders have equally affable and genuine people around them.

Mind you, it took me a while to get to know them. The noise from the crowd, and from the cursed public-address system, made conversation very difficult and I just exchanged pleasantries with a pleasant middle-aged lady and her daughter who sat in the row behind me. And then, just after Christmas 2008, I suddenly stopped going! And I didn't attend again until April 2009.

Had I lost interest, after so many years attending home matches? No, certainly not! But I thought I had better write to the two ladies to explain why I hadn't made an appearance for so long, in case they were worried. And so, I sent them a letter via the club, explaining to the club where the two ladies sat, saying I fully understood that the club couldn't pass on the ladies' address to me but asking them if they could possibly forward my letter on to them. The result was that, a week or two later, a lovely letter came back from the two ladies. They told me they lived in Newport and said that everyone around me had been most worried by my prolonged absence and they hoped I would be able to return soon. How kind it was of the club to pass on my letter.

What had happened was this: I had gone for a walk on Cannock Chase four days after Christmas to keep my body in shape. I decided to walk from Milford Common to The Glacial Boulder, brought down to its current position, high on the Chase above Sherbrook Valley, by glacial flow in the last Ice Age. I would be walking for about two miles to the boulder and then retracing my tracks to my car on the Common. And so, it would be a good, hilly, four miles constitutional to work off Christmas indulgence.

The day was quite mild but it had been very cold over the holiday period and mud lay on top of thawing ice and snow, but my climbing boots and walking pole kept me on an even keel. I made it to the boulder, precariously perched above Sherbrook valley. I returned across the plateau and up and then down the long drag, without incident. That is, until I was within half a mile of Milford Common, with some undulating walking between me and the warm sanctuary of my car. And then it happened - I put my heel down, skidded on a piece of muddy ice, flew up in the air and fell heavily on my right shoulder. A searing pain shot through my right arm as I lay there, wondering how I was going to get up. It was past 3.30pm, there was nobody around and darkness was closing in. A cold night beckoned.

The only way to get up was to push with my injured right arm. The pain was indescribable but I had to bear it - I wouldn't have survived a night out on the Chase, and I had to get up so that I could access my phone, trapped underneath me in my trousers pocket. My arm hung by my side like a useless lump of jelly as I crept slowly and gingerly along, each step jarring my arm agonisingly, aiming for the road rather than risking the walk over the hills in the gathering gloom. Once on the road I found a lamp post and summoned my wife by its light. Ten minutes later she and my daughter arrived, just as I reached the Common, and she drove me home in my car, my daughter following in hers.

Two very nice female paramedics enthused over the multi-coloured bruising of my arm and then administered a dose of laughing gas to ease the pain. "Is it working?" they asked in the ambulance that sped me to hospital. "Well I feel as if I've just been down the pub and had four pints," I replied. "It's working!" they declared.

The upshot was that I had fractured my humerus, just below the shoulder, and severely damaged my shoulder ligaments. The bone surgeon who examined me next day was a bundle of fun:

"Is it painful?" he asked;

"Yes!" I replied;

"Well, it'll get a lot worse before it gets better," he reassured me breezily.

Yes, and I hope you have a very happy New Year too!

Recuperation was slow and painful and I had to sleep in an armchair for two weeks. Whilst I was recovering (with a series of sessions of excruciating physiotherapy) I was diagnosed with osteoporosis - so the childhood rickets had left its legacy after all.

I made it back to my seat by April, in time to celebrate the promotion triumph of Mick McCarthy's team as we closed it off with narrow wins against QPR and Doncaster Rovers. This time I didn't dance on the pitch, as it was rather a long way down from the Steve Bull Upper, and I didn't want to do-in my other shoulder. Our joy knew no bounds - once more back in the

Premier League, and determined to stay there this time.

I became firm friends with the Newport mother and daughter, and we would meet for a coffee before home matches, where we were able to converse easily, away from the tannoy din. Over the next few years they drove me to away matches at Wigan, Bolton, Rotherham, Milton Keynes and Preston. It was with great pleasure that I invited them into my box as special guests for my swan song treat organised by Wolves.

The last couple of years, as I grew less steady on my feet, I found it more and more difficult to descend the steps leading down to my seat, one row from the front. So, this year I reluctantly moved my seat higher up so that I wouldn't have to descend so many steps. Incidentally, I had written to Mr Moxey, pointing out that we needed a handrail like the one easily visible in the new Stan Cullis Stand - but answer came there none. Obviously, helping Parkies not to topple from top to bottom of the stand was not high on his priority list, and nor was courtesy either, by the look of it.

My new seat didn't last long; I could see my mates who were below me, way down the stand and I was totally bereft and longing to be back with them (I think I spoke no more than a dozen words to those around me in my new seat). After only two matches I had transferred my seat back amongst my friends again.

The very last time I took up my seat I had to ask for a steward's assistance to get me down to it. And that, I'm afraid, is that. I won't be taking up my seat again next time. My season ticket days are over. But they were wonderful times while they lasted.

Chapter 22
Some of
My Favourite Players

A better centre half than Wright
You won't find, searching day or night.

Then moving on a little later,
Who could be better than Bill Slater?

And looking round for hours and hours,
You won't find one to match Ron Flowers.

Now, woe betide whoever flew at
the resolute, hard Eddie Stuart.

Of tough men, Edwin is the champ;
He tackles hard - one Eddie Clamp.

Opposing forwards found no fun
in facing Malcolm Finlayson.

Did strikers score goals in a hurry?
Not if our man in goal was Murray.

In London, Dusseldorf or Paris,
Do fullbacks play like Gerry Harris?

With Broadbent, Mullen, Deeley, Bull,
Our cup of joy is brimming full.

I could just get out my Wolves bible and go through the players I have seen, one by one, but I won't do that. Instead, I'll describe the players who have given me especial pleasure over the years and whose names stand out in my memory.

———————

The first name on every team sheet, as they say, must be **Billy Wright**, peerless and magnificent. I started watching Wolves in 1957-58 and was privileged enough to see him play out his final two seasons. Some say he was declining by then, but if what I saw was a player in decline, then I would have loved to have seen him in his prime. He retired before season 1959-60 kicked-off, having found pre-season training too arduous; the players would undertake punishing training runs over the Cannock Chase hills as part of their pre-season training, and Wright couldn't keep up - he was out of puff. He realised his fitness wasn't up to it anymore; it was nothing to do with a decline in ability. (I can vouch for the severity of those hills above Milford Common).

It was an iconic sight to see the blonde, curly-haired Billy leading the team out at a trot (the players didn't amble out in those days), the ball in his hand, an expression on his face which said we're here to do as good a job as we can, but we respect the opposition and will try to play within the spirit of the rules. Above all, he was modest, and a gentleman through and through.

He was a rock in defence and seemed to possess springs in his heels. When the ball needed heading away, Wright would be the last to rise, and he seemed to hang in the air. His timing was superb, and to see his head in contact with the ball as his opponents were back on the ground, their jumps having been completed, was a marvel to behold. He was a peer among peers.

I will mention **Jimmy Mullen** next because, like Billy Wright, he completed his career during the season 1958-59 and I saw a good bit of his last two years. It is a great regret of mine that I didn't start attending matches as a younger schoolboy and so missed his great partnership with little Johnny Hancocks. However, I enjoyed his pairing with little Norman Deeley instead. Jimmy was quite a tall man, in comparison with his partner on the other flank, and he possessed the hardest left foot shot I have ever seen (yes, even harder than Alan Hinton's). Lay the ball nicely on his left foot within sight of goal (see my description of the 1957 Everton match) and - WHOOOMF! - the ball was rearranging the back of the net.

There was a match against Birmingham City on 25th October 1958, which I shall call the Mullen / Merricks show, and for good reason. Gill Merricks was an outstanding goalie for Birmingham, and he could pull off unbelievable saves. On the day in question he had to, as Mullen spent his afternoon peppering Gill's goal with a fusillade of ferocious shots - on another day, against a lesser goalie, Mullen would have scored six -

while Merricks spent HIS afternoon pulling off a series of fabulous saves to thwart Jimmy. Mullen managed to pierce his defences twice, to set up a 3-1 win and, at the end, the two players warmly embraced, recognising the sheer brilliance and professionalism in each other.

Eddie Stuart and **Gerry Harris** were the Morecambe & Wise of the Wolves defence, not because they were funny men but because they worked so well together, making up a formidable pair of full backs. Both tough-tackling, Eddie was the real hard man and gave as good as he got. He bravely migrated from South Africa, when only 19, to sign for Wolves, won two trophies for them and was granted the supreme honour of succeeding the great Billy Wright as skipper of the team. However, loss of form saw Bill Slater take over this role and, sadly, Eddie missed out on what would have been a richly deserved FA Cup winner's medal in 1960.

Gerry Harris controlled the left flank of Wolves' defence, and not much got through. In fact, he and Stuart did their job so well that, in the championship winning seasons of 1957-58 and 1958-59, and while the forwards were scoring centuries of goals, they conceded fewer than 50 goals on each occasion.

Cullis didn't like his defence to play too square and this scared me a bit when one of the full backs moved into the centre to cover his colleague, in case he was skinned by the opposing winger. This left a big gap on the other flank, into which the opposing winger on that side ran and picked up the pass. But the full backs then reversed their roles, one going out to meet his winger while the other covered for him in the middle. It worked well, as evidenced by the results. Maybe Stuart and Harris gambled on the opposing winger not crossing the ball, knowing that Wright would head it away all day long; the opposing winger's only other option was to beat the fullback, but Stuart and Harris were ready for that tactic, providing double cover against a dribbling winger.

Behind these two, and providing a formidable last line of defence was big, fearless **Malcolm Finlayson**. He was certainly a very big man and very brave too, throwing himself at opposition feet on many occasions, but also capable of launching his huge frame skywards to make some fabulous saves. I recall one out-of-this-world save that saw him twist and change direction in the air to tip a goal-bound shot over the bar - I think it was against Barcelona in the European Cup (I also saw Geoff Sidebottom pull off a similar save as he changed direction in mid-air to deny West Brom's Derek Kevan a goal).

Decades later, **Matt Murray** was our keeper, but for a tragically brief spell. He was another very big man and his height and frame put undue pressure on his knees. He was a hero for us in the Play-Off final of 2003, saving a second half penalty, when Sheffield were threatening to get back into the game but, sadly, he was unable to enjoy the Premier League season that followed and was forced.to retire in his prime. Not once was he heard to moan or complain about his misfortune. He is an example to us all and a credit to humanity.

A third goalie I had a lot of time for was **Phil Parkes**, another giant of a man, and seemingly ever-present during the late 60s and into the 70s. He gave the club great service and was, I believe, behind only the great Bert Williams in the number of appearances he totted up between the "sticks".

Our current guardian of the goals is another giant of a man, **Carl Ikeme**, not a particularly bulky person, but very tall indeed. He has made the position his own and is, in my estimation, a very fine goalie. Still comparatively young for a keeper, he has many years left to show what he can do for the Wolves cause.

It sounds as if all our goalkeepers were giants but Noel Dwyer and Geoff Sidebottom (mentioned above) were quite small men in comparison to the big guys.

———————

The great half backs **Bill Slater**, **Ron Flowers** and **Eddie Clamp**, together with Billy Wright, made up an all-Wolves half back line for England, in various combinations of any three from four, Wright and Flowers in turn captaining their country. For a club to have four internationals to choose from for three positions was quite remarkable, back in the 50s.

I've already mentioned the cultured Slater, taking over from Wright, Stuart and George Showell at centre half and bringing a new style and finesse to the position. If I dare say it, he was almost as good on the ball as Peter Broadbent and he scored some good goals when playing at wing half or inside forward.

A word about George Showell - his unenviable task was to deputise for Billy Wright when the latter was away on international duty. When Wright wasn't playing for England, Showell couldn't get into the team, and so he played few games. But he never complained and never let the team down when called upon. He became the regular right back when Stuart moved to Stoke City and received his just rewards in 1960, when he was a member of the FA Cup winning team.

But the dynamo in that 50s half back line was the immense Ron Flowers, a colossus of a man, both in size and influence, and vying with Mullen, Hancocks, Wharton, Hinton and Sako for title of hardest hitter of the ball. I've talked about his special in the 9-0 annihilation of Fulham in 1959 (which I didn't see) and I've also seem him score some snorters myself. But perhaps his most spectacular goal came in the match against Leicester City, also in 1959. A high ball down the middle was met by the soaring Flowers and he directed a magnificent header into the top corner of the net, with the goalie beaten all ends up. Unfortunately, the goalie's name was Malcolm Finlayson and Flowers had scored in his own net - but it was a goal to savour, nevertheless.

Eddie Clamp was our hard man, but not especially dirty, and certainly not to be compared with a certain notorious member of a later Wolves team. But he was the one whom away crowds loved to hate, as he gave no quarter and got in some crunching tackles. He had a terrific shot on him and I remember a grass-trimmer of a shot from all of 40 yards which arrowed into the net in the 5-0 championship decider against Luton Town in 1959.

The enduring image I have of Clamp comes from a match against Manchester United. Bobby Charlton was away down the middle, his lock of hair flowing out behind him. Clamp couldn't reach him to tackle him or even bring him down. Nothing daunted, he improvised by hitching a lift on Charlton's back. Bobby found himself carrying Clamp piggyback style for some yards, before the ref brought an end to the proceedings. I can't recall whether the two shook hands or not, but I don't think Mr Charlton was particularly impressed by the close attentions of Mr Clamp.

———————

From that truly great 50s forward line I've already extolled the virtues of **Norman Deeley, Peter Broadbent, Jimmy Murray** and **Jimmy Mullen**. The only one from my first match, **Dennis Wilshaw**, whom I haven't mentioned, played just twice in my presence before leaving for Stoke City, so I can't express an opinion on him. His successor was **Bobby Mason**, a skilful player who could control the ball closely whilst running at top speed. He had a good goals-to-appearances ratio but was notorious for missing what would have been the 10th goal in the dying seconds of that marvellous Fulham match. He was another regular to sadly miss out on a place in the FA Cup winning side of 1960. The young Barry Stobart was preferred to Bobby in that match.

The side I first watched on 2nd November 1957, was: **Finlayson, Stuart, Harris, Clamp, Wright, Flowers,**

Deeley, Broadbent, Murray, Wilshaw, Mullen and, of that team, all but Harris and Flowers have passed on to the celestial Molineux above - a sad passing of a wonderful team.

Chapter 23
Parkinson's Awareness

Although my health is often poor, and sometimes fairly grotty,
We nonetheless flew out last year to rocky Lanzarote.

We sought assistance with our luggage, getting on the train,
but managed easily enough to board the aeroplane.

I need some leg-room, so we book a gangway seat for me.
My wife is there as well, but tagging on is Mr P.

I should have said "Get lost you pest. Good riddance and goodbye".
But still this parasite is with us, way up in the sky.

Our seaside chalet is palatial, up there with the best,
But straightaway it's clear we have an uninvited guest.

That evil P. upon my back, a parasitic rotter,
He'll ruin our stay, and plague us both - a most unwelcome squatter.

Essentially, he rules our lives; he's nothing but a leech,
as he pursues us from the chalet down onto the beach.

*It's really very difficult to know what irks us most
as he pursues us closely as we walk along the coast.*

*I have some trouble with my balance, causing me to sway,
But I can't get relief because he just won't go away.*

*He's with me in the shop and so I drop my change and fumble.
Then all the other shoppers have a moan, and tut and grumble.*

*I'm at the checkout - so is he! The queue comes to a stop.
I dither over paying and I'm holding up the shop.*

*I go on an excursion and decide to take the bus.
He gets on too and flusters me - which makes the driver cuss!*

*He's just attention-seeking, so I'll show him I don't care.
I'll totally ignore him and pretend he isn't there.*

*I'll be less introspective and won't dwell as much on me.
By thinking happy thoughts, then I won't think of Mr P.*

*I'll probably still sway and stumble, whisper, choke and drool,
But these are minor problems and don't matter much at all.*

*I'll focus on my wife instead and think of what she needs;
So rather than be selfish I'll assist with loving deeds.*

For up to now she's cared for me and so it's only fair

I LOVE TO GO A WANDERING

that I, in turn, give her a bit of tender, loving care.

One night we were quite hungry and we went out on the hunt
for wholesome food and drink as we progressed along the front.

The weather was most pleasant and exceptionally warm,
There was no hint that soon there'd be the most-almighty storm.

But suddenly a vicious wind blew debris in the air,
and carried it above the waves, depositing it there.

We needed to escape the wind and find some safe, warm shelter,
But we could find none and just panicked, running helter-skelter.

Now, as we tried to beat the gale, some sand blew in her eye;
It was so harsh and painful that it almost made her cry.

She wears a pair of contact lenses and it makes her fret
when gritty sand gets in behind them, causing great upset.

She clung to me in desperation, both her eyes unseeing;
Just one solution left to us - maintain our frantic fleeing.

It seemed like several hours before I led her from the storm,
inside a friendly restaurant - a refuge safe and warm.

We were aware someone was missing - it was Mr P.,
We wished him ill, and hoped that he'd been blown well out to sea.

We rested well, enjoyed our food and then went on our way;
The storm had gone, and we'd enjoyed a splendid holiday.

My loving wife's been always there, forever at my side;
We've walked and shopped and sunbathed and enjoyed a camel ride.

Volcanoes we have visited and handled red-hot lava -
a lot more fun than being trapped by Mr P.'s palaver.

For Mr. P is nothing - he's pathetic, mean and small,
While Chris and I are very different - we feel ten feet tall.

A friend and helper, wife and guide - all these to me she's been;
She is my bulwark and my strength - the rock on which I lean.

As sure as night and sunrise and as certain as the tide,
In joy and hardship - she'll be there - forever at my side.

I'll just say this to Mr P - do give yourself a break.
Just stay out here and keep away from us, for goodness' sake.

In Lanzarote you can stay; in sun or wind or rain,
And may our paths be never blighted by your face again.

Feel free to eat and shop and swim and drink and walk and roam.
You won't encounter us again - we're shortly going home.

From this day on I'll be upbeat and be a little bolder.
I will enjoy my life, now I've dislodged you from my shoulder.

The above lines paint an optimistic picture and it's good to be positive about Parkinson's, but I'm afraid it will probably get you in the end. However, we all die of something, so why not make the most of life while we still have it?

We await with bated breath a breakthrough in research which will arrest and, hopefully, reverse the condition, but will it come in my lifetime? I have hope and faith that it will.

The national charity for research into Parkinson's Disease, Parkinson's UK, urges all "Parkies" to bring awareness of the condition to their friends and acquaintances. As a fully-fledged member of the Parkie guild myself, I unashamedly use this chapter to do just that.

I have already explained briefly what Parkinson's is; namely, a deficiency of dopamine neurons in the brain, which leads to difficulties with movement and locomotion (moving around). How does Parkinson's manifest itself?

There are about 125,000 people who suffer from Parkinson's Disease (PD) in the UK and a total of ten million in the world. They say everyone's PD is different and unique to that individual, so that's a great number of different manifestations of the condition. How, then, does it affect me?

For a start, you might not think I have the disease because I'm not troubled by the shakes. It is a common misconception that all Parkies suffer from tremors or shakes, but many do not. My mother had such severe shaking hands that you could hear her coming with a cup of tea, as the cup rattled away merrily in the saucer. However, she didn't pass this annoying disability on to me. I first detected my own embryonic PD through my running, so it's perhaps as well I took up the sport as it turned out to be a diagnostic tool; and the earlier the diagnosis is made, the more likely the disease's progression can be delayed and slowed.

I started getting pains at the top of my quadriceps muscle in the right leg when I ran, and I had to stop to massage the offending spot to ease the pain. After a while, my leg would suddenly twitch and jerk outwards and, on one occasion, it threw me to the ground. This was somewhat alarming and I went to my physio for advice, thinking I might have a trapped nerve or something similar. Finding nothing, she referred me on to my chiropractor. She found nothing either and so I ended up having a consultation with a neurologist who, after first doubting that I had the condition, finally decided that I did, in fact, suffer from mild PD.

Normally, on receiving such a diagnosis, one does not fully appreciate the significance of it because of the general ignorance concerning the condition. However, I was more knowledgeable than most people, being aware from my mum's illness what to expect and so I was poleaxed for a while by the news. However, after a period of what might be called mourning, I decided to fight Mr PD and get on with my life. Hence, I attempted to climb Kilimanjaro one more time, took up table tennis again, introduced indoor short-mat bowling, tai chi and chess into my life, and bought a season ticket for Wolves. The PD progressed quite slowly until this year, when it appears that, after forcing itself to struggle up a steep hill, with me straining vigorously to resist, it seems to have crested the brow and to be now freewheeling merrily down the other side and carrying me to eventual and inevitable perdition.

General symptoms, common to all, or most, Parkies are slowness of movement, difficulty with fiddly actions, such as doing up buttons and tying shoelaces, softening of speech and ungainly walking. I exhibit all these characteristics, together with some others, which can be embarrassing and distressing.

For instance, I suffer from excessive drooling and find myself having to constantly mop my mouth with tissues. Once, when on a plane, I leant across the seat to point out something to a stranger and dribbled on his book. We all produce saliva, which we swallow about every 10 seconds or so. The Parkie's swallowing reflex is compromised and he or she forgets to swallow - the result is that the saliva dribbles out of the mouth, instead of going down the throat. This problem can be exacerbated by the sufferer having difficulties with the swallowing reflex in any case.

So, when I eat out, I avoid highly coloured foods, such as tomato soup, knowing they will certainly colour my beard. On balance, I think it best to retain my facial hair, to mop up the flow a little, rather than let it drip straight off my bare chin.

PD can affect the bowels, as it does mine, quickening their action or slowing things down. Access to a toilet is essential, and then a further difficulty occurs - having to fiddle with buttons and zips.

And a very awkward and embarrassing effect of PD arises from its effects on the facial muscles. They lose their elasticity and the face becomes expressionless and zombie-like, as if one is wearing a mask. People don't know what you're thinking because you don't show it in your face, and this can lead to unfortunate misunderstandings, particularly if you are attempting to crack a joke. Your deadpan expression can lead them to think you are being serious, and this can result in anger or even resentment. As a result, a Parkie's slowness of action and lack of expression can make other people think they are a bit of an unfriendly idiot, when quite the reverse is probably true - they want to be friendly but are having trouble with all their muscles, and they don't talk very loudly. If the public were aware of these things then tolerance and understanding would surely be the happy result.

I often think that, although Parkies may appear to be a little bit like automatons, the exact opposite is, in fact, the case. Nothing is automatic anymore and every movement needs to be thought about - "Now I put this foot forward with the opposite arm, then the other foot with this arm, etc." Walking needs to be relearned as if one were a baby again, and the same with other actions. There aren't enough neurons left to function as before. Coping strategies need to be learned and it's all somewhat frustrating. However, one reflex remains, and will never disappear—the reflex to rise from one's seat and throw one's arms in the air and let out a bellow when Wolves score a goal! Most Parkies can manage that - well, the ones that support the Wolves at least.

Until just recently I was driving my car, but now I have lost confidence and use public transport if my wife isn't able to chauffeur me. I would travel to matches at Molineux by bus and train, walking the final three quarters of a mile from the railway station to the ground, but finding it increasingly difficult to coordinate my walking. A typical journey to Wolves from Little Haywood would have been as follows:

Get dressed and make sure I know where everything is to be found - bus pass, senior railcard, money for train ticket, newspaper, food and match programme - oh, and season ticket to get into the ground. And, of course, have access to a plentiful supply of tissues to mop up the dribble. Fiddling for these things later would be disastrous and I find cold weather better than warm, insofar as I will be wearing lots of clothes with lots of pockets in which to stow things. On the other hand, I have become intolerant of the cold and find myself shivering before the end of an afternoon match on a winter's day. Evening winter matches have become a definite no-no for me in the past year or so.

Walking to the ground from the station became more and more difficult and embarrassing, as my body grew increasingly stooped and forward-leaning, and my stride grew short and rapid as I chased my own feet as I tried to keep up with my centre of gravity. Eventually, I decided I couldn't cope any longer, but a temporary reprieve was at hand.

My good friend from our village table tennis club discovered that I was an avid Wolves supporter, and she also found out about my disability. She and her husband, both fanatical Wolves fans themselves, generously offered to squeeze me into their car on match days. They, like me, are season ticket holders in the Steve Bull Stand and they have a regular parking space about a quarter of a mile from the ground. I joyfully accepted their offer, but I lasted only two more matches before I had to call it a day.

I've already mentioned that Jez Moxey didn't consider it necessary to respond to my request for a handrail to assist people like me descend the steps to the lower rows - I'm sure he had the best interests of the fans at heart and mustn't have received my email. Anyway, I was finding the descent very scary as I placed my left foot, pointing sideways, on the next step down, followed by placing the right foot on the same step, and then on to the next step in the same manner, and so on until, eventually and agonisingly, I reached my row, two from the front. I then had to squeeze past all the people between me and my seat, bang in the middle of the row, without toppling into the row below. But people were extraordinarily kind, standing up and squeezing themselves against their seat to give me space. But reluctantly, after two lifts to Molineux, I had to tell my friends I would have to call it a day.

The last match I attended with them was the Aston Villa derby, which we happily won. However, this wasn't my final game at Molineux after all—there was to be one more match to come, and I'll tell you about it in a later chapter.

That's my PD lesson over and we can get back to all things pertaining to Wolves.

Chapter 24
Keeping Fit

You'll likely spark domestic wars
if you do exercise indoors.

You'll probably get frowns and glares,
Performing step-ups on the stairs.

And she won't like it if you zoom,
a lot of laps, around the room.

For each accumulated mile
will flatten down the carpet pile.

Some say "tomarto", some "tomayto";
You're safest as a couch potato!

In 2010, Wolves' first season in the Premier League under Mick McCarthy, I thought it was high time I introduced some fitness training back into my life, after being away from running for so long.

It is very important for a PD sufferer (a Parkie) to maintain as much physical fitness as they can, so that the progress of the condition is slowed down. Mental fitness is also important, so sending silly ditties and verses to message boards and blogs, and writing rambling accounts of one's Wolves-supporting experiences keep the mind alert and lessen the danger of dementia setting in.

Since I broke my arm in 2008 and was diagnosed as having osteoporosis I was very cautious about falling over and of breaking further bones, and so indoor exercise seemed the best bet. I've described how I took up table tennis (TT) again, and introduced indoor short-mat bowls, both of which I seemed quite adept at, throwing myself around in TT and not falling over. Bowls was more sedate, but was very enjoyable, and Tai Chi is reckoned to exercise every muscle in the body - so all good activities to undertake. However, as an ex-athlete, I felt the need for something more vigorous to get the heart pumping and enable me to continue getting down to the Wolves regularly, and so I decided to do a daily dose of step-ups.

Each day I would step up and down on the bottom stair, a height of 20 centimetres, and I built up to a total of 600 step-ups in a session, in a fast time of 22 minutes, so that was about 25 to 30 step-ups in a minute. I reckon that, when I gave up the step-ups in 2012, I had climbed the height of Kilimanjaro and more, and so I did finally make it to the top!

Crazy, you might think, and you might well be right. But even more bizarre was what followed. I eventually abandoned the step-ups because they were affecting my back and giving me sciatica, so what could I do in their place? I had accompanied my wife to cross country races to support her (and to make amends for the selfishness of Portsmouth - see Chapter Eight!) and I had done a little light jogging on the soft grass without mishap, so maybe I could try gentle running again. But I didn't want any falls. How about, then, if I did some indoor running, instead, in our lounge, on a soft carpet, falling into armchairs if I lost my balance, and needing to run only 92 laps to complete a mile? Just what the doctor ordered - I didn't hear you say stark raving bonkers, did I?

I carried on with this running for two years, building up to a maximum of six miles in a session (a bit mind-numbing, having to count 552 laps) and in the two years up to 2013 I covered 1,307 miles. Not many people have run more than a thousand miles round their lounges; not many have counted 120,244 laps in the process - not many are stupid enough, you may say - but I reckon I'm a world record holder for running around lounges, so there!

This running was keeping me very fit, but I eventually had to stop it because of knee problems. Back in my 50s I had had a wash out of the debris in my knee under keyhole surgery, and the same knee was complaining again so, short of undergoing another operation, it was curtains for me as far as running was concerned. As a result, my fitness fell away and my walks from Wolverhampton station to the football stadium became more awkward and clumsy.

Mind you, I was quite quick and nimble for my age and condition in catching the train back home on time. The match usually finished at 4.50 or 4.55pm, I would applaud the players off the pitch, have a quick glance at the scores on the TV monitor on the concourse and then leg it into the subway. The crowd generally moved at a good pace through the subway, and there wasn't much danger of falling over in that mass of humanity. Then it was up the steps, keeping a good grasp of the handrail, before dodging through the crowds at a good pace, past the university and on past the Grand Theatre and the bus station to the trains, generally arriving with two or three minutes to spare. I can no longer manage this.

Five pleasant gentlemen to my right in the stand - I call it octogenarian row -would regularly rise from their seats five minutes before the match ended and depart, regardless of the match situation. Perhaps they had an earlier train to catch, or a long walk to their cars, or just wished to beat the traffic away - I have no wish to judge them. I have left early on just the one occasion, for a good reason which I have explained earlier in the book. If you can't remember the occasion, or the reason for the early exit, and it's bugging you, then you will have to read the book again! No, I'm only joking; it's in Chapter 17!

Before the match, in the early days of my season ticket tenure, I would have a pint in the "Moon" and soak up the atmosphere but later, as alcohol didn't mix well with the PD medication I was on, I would have a coffee in Costa's with the lady and her daughter from Newport. After putting the world, and Wolves, to rights we would saunter along to take up our seats in the Steve Bull stand. Those were very pleasant days.

Chapter 25
More of
My Favourite Players

You must be absolutely barkin'
to rate as worthless, Derek Parkin.

And no one would consider lightly
the task of marking Michael Kightly.

Opponents found it quite a blow
When facing Bobby Woodruff's throw.

It must have worried any Baggie
We had a winger good as Waggy.

Ron Saunders was a little dull,
To sell us striker, Stevie Bull.

He kicked himself for every score;
Three hundred kicks, and then six more!

I can't possibly mention all the players I have seen and admired at Wolves, so I will continue describing my favourite players, taken from a random selection - it is inevitable, of course, that certain players must be included, whether chosen randomly or not.

One of the prime nominees is **Derek Parkin**, a left back who played for us for nigh on 14 years and whose total of 609 appearances was quite staggering, and, more than any other Wolves player in history. He played through the 70s and was a skilful, dependable and classy full back. His nickname was Squeak, because of the high register of his north-eastern voice, although I never heard it from the enclosures.

Before his time, in the 60s, came his predecessor at left back, **Bobby Thomson**, probably the most cultured full back I have seen. He was extremely fast and I have seen him streak down the flank in pursuit of an opposition winger who had got a fair head-start on him, rob the winger and then turn and hare off with the ball in the opposite direction. Bobby, it was, who scored one of the two late goals that saved us from shame and defeat in a cup tie at Oldham (see Chapter 10).

The other of those two face-saving goals was scored by **Mike Bailey**, an inspirational attacking midfielder and skipper, who drove the team forward by sheer force of character and by self-example. He was often described as being barrel-chested. Now, I don't know what that cliché means, but he had big lungs and a big heart, and he used them to the full in the service of Wolves. He captained Wolves both to the UEFA Cup finals and to the League Cup Wembley triumph against Manchester City in 1974.

A rock in defence alongside him was **Frank Munro**, a giant of a defender who served us faithfully for nearly 10 years. Mountaineers talk of bagging "Munros" (mountains over 3000 feet in height); well, we certainly bagged our own Munro and what an acquisition he turned out to be. He scored some crucial goals, too, but was cruelly struck down by illness when he retired.

A terrific midfielder / winger, who served us for over 15 years, was **Kenny Hibbitt**. His appearances record of 574 matches was bettered only by Derek Parkin. He scored 114 goals, most of them lashing shots, the most memorable being the opening goal in the 1974 League Cup win. He was an incredible player and an incredible servant.

On the 7th March 1964 Wolves played Birmingham City at Molineux. Just 16,000 hardy souls turned up towards the end of a season in which Wolves would win just 12 times and would finish 18th - worse, much worse, was to follow a year on from then. Pleasingly, they won that day 5-1, but the crowd was in for a shock - a pleasant shock, as it turned out. A new player, one **Bobby Woodruff**, had been signed from unfashionable Swindon Town. Nobody had heard of him, but he was making his debut that day. He picked the ball up to take a throw in, and there was a collective gasp from 16,000 throats, as he launched the ball through the air. I swear he was standing close to the halfway line when he delivered the throw and the ball reached the penalty spot, a distance of at least 40 yards - eat your heart out, Rory Delap! Never had such a prodigious throw been witnessed at Molineux (though it must have been seen at Swindon a time or two). Woodruff was an instant hero and this weapon in his armoury proved most valuable to us.

Wingers often come in pairs - Hancocks and Mullen, for instance, or Wharton and Hinton, but others seem to plough a lone furrow, picking up partners as they go. Deeley, for instance, didn't have a regular partner, but operated in turn with Mullen, Mannion, Lill and Des Horne. A player in a similar situation was **David Wagstaffe**, and he enjoyed fruitful partnerships with Terry Wharton, Jim McCalliog and Kenny Hibbitt, amongst others, in his long and imperious reign, marauding down Wolves' left wing.

Waggy, as he was affectionately known by fans, didn't have the happiest of introductions to Molineux, as he was one of the unfortunate recipients of the 8-1 thrashing Wolves handed out to Manchester City at the start of the 1962-63 campaign. But two years later he was our player, staying for 12 seasons and picking up a League Cup winner's medal in 1974. Of all the Wolves' wingers that I have seen he was, quite simply, the best. He had mesmerising skills and could turn an opponent inside out, dodging this way and that, before delivering the perfect cross for Dougan or Richards to despatch into the back of the net. What wouldn't Bully have given for his services! He might have scored 500 goals. Waggy had a good shot on him himself and scored some crackers. When he left us in 1976 he had played over 400 matches and scored 31 goals - a genius in the Peter Broadbent mould.

Terry Wharton and **Alan Hinton** were an exciting pair of young wingers who first came together in season 1961-62 and were part of the 8-1 demolition job just mentioned, the two of them scoring in that match.

Hinton was fast and racy down the wing and could put in telling centres when at full speed or facing away from goal - in the Jimmy Mullen mould. He had a ferocious left foot shot, again like Mullen. It is a very close call for me in deciding the best left winger of my 60 years of supporting our great team, but Waggy's ball skills just have the edge over Hinton and Mullen's speed, crossing and shooting.

Terry Wharton was also fast and he had a murderous right foot shot (see Chapter 10 for a description of his goal in the match against Sheffield United). Wharton was a brave player, not easily put off his game, whereas Hinton allowed the crowd to get to him. Shamefully, they drove him away after four short years, but he had the last laugh, playing for Nottingham Forest and Derby County, under Brian Clough, and winning Championship medals with the latter club. Wharton was strong enough to be able to tough it out at Wolves for 10 years before moving to the other Wanderers at Bolton.

Michael Kightly and **Matt Jarvis** comprised a pair of wingers very much in the Wharton/ Hinton mould. Kightly was fast and exciting, with a big shot on him, whereas Jarvis had great pace and the ability to skin his full back, before delivering crosses for the strikers to deal with. Sadly, both moved on to higher things when Wolves fell through the divisions in the 2010s.

Mention must be made of one more winger - **Steve Kindon**. He was built like a Tank and, indeed, took that appellation as a nickname. He must have struck terror into opponents when he ran at them; it was often said in jest that, if the North Bank gates had been opened when he was charging in that direction, he would have reached Gailey Roundabout before coming to a halt.

And so, we come to the strikers. Everybody has their own personal favourite, although it is clear what the majority verdict would be regarding the best Wolves striker of all time. But I hereby declare that **Hughie McIlmoyle** - no, please no. Don't lynch me! Pick the book out of the bin and read on. You didn't let me finish. What I was about to say was that McIlmoyle was the best striker, as far as heading of the ball is concerned, that I have seen. He could climb even higher than Derek Dougan to flick the ball on, and seemed to hang in the air like Billy Wright. That's all I was going to say. I hope that's cleared that up. Have you got the book back from the bin yet?

Incidentally, McIlmoyle had the best song of all the strikers. To the tune of the refrain of "She'll be coming down the mountains when she comes [that is, 'singing aye, aye, yippee, yippee aye']" the choir would chant:

> *Singing aye, aye Hughie McIlmoyle;*
> *Singing aye, aye Hughie McIlmoyle;*
> *Singing aye, aye Hughie; aye, aye Hughie;*
> *Aye, aye Hughie McIlmoyle.*

His name just fitted into the line perfectly, without any wrenching of the metre to accommodate it.

From all those I have seen my candidates for best striker ever, in strict alphabetical order, are **Steve Bull, Derek Dougan, Jimmy Murray** and **John Richards**. I will discuss each one in historical order.

Before I do that, let's compare the scoring records of the four contenders:

Murray, with 166 goals from 299 matches has the best record averaged out, with a ratio of 1.801 games per goal;

Bull has 306 goals from 561 matches (ratio 1.833);

Richards has 194 goals from 486 matches (ratio 2.505);

Dougan has 123 goals from 323 matches (ratio 2.526).

Murray and Bull are very close, but Murray played only just over half the number of games that Bull did. Would he have kept up his high scoring average if he had played another 300 games? It's very difficult to say, and statistics alone won't give the answer. Once again, it comes down to opinion and gut feeling.

As an aside, consider a striker who has an even lower games-to-goals ratio than Bull and Murray; Ted Farmer scored 42 goals from 62 appearances, before he had to retire at the tragically young age of 24. His average of 1.409 games per goal would, if he had gone on to play as many games as Bull at the same rate of scoring, have seen him retire with 398 goals under his belt. But he didn't, and we can't predict what would have happened. However, what a talent was lost by Wolves.

I watched Jimmy Murray during his peak years and was highly impressed by him. He led the line superbly and was highly instrumental in helping his team lift three major trophies. A slightly built player, he was a natural goal scorer.

Derek Dougan was a maverick, a law unto himself and thrilling to watch. He formed a lethal partnership with John Richards and was superb at rising and flicking the ball through with his head for his strike partner to run on to; he also scored many crucial goals himself. And who could have scored a hat-trick on his home debut with more flamboyance than did the Doog? He got into some scrapes in his time and, on one occasion, managed to get himself suspended for an eight-match period.

John Richards was the epitome of grace, speed and power, with an uncanny knack of knowing where the goal was. His party piece was to receive the ball with his back to goal, turn in a flash and streak past his marker to find the back of the net. He was class personified and a superb striker. It was a disgrace that he was selected just once for England, and that out of position on the wing and purely as a concession to the clamour from the Midlands for his inclusion. If you don't play in London then your international career is compromised.

The exploits of the final striker on the list, Bully, are still fresh in most of our memories. What an amazing bargain Ron Saunders gifted to us - bless him - and how phenomenally he transformed our fortunes, from the pits of the 4th division to a position knocking on the door of the Premier League. His record of two tallies of 50 goals in successive seasons was stupendous and unprecedented, and he totally eclipsed John Richards' club record of 194 goals with a never-to-be-beaten 306 goals. His record won't ever be beaten because players just aren't loyal enough anymore to stay at one club long enough to do it. His great regret is that he did not have a chance to shine at the highest level of club football, but this was down to the club's deficiencies and not to his own shortcomings. Indeed, he could have moved to gain Premiership status, but chose to remain loyal to his first love, Wolves. He is one in a million.

Some people scoff because his mountain of goals was not scored in the top division, but that is utter rubbish. He scored at the very highest level, for his country, for ENGLAND, and you don't get any higher than that.

Since his retirement, from knees worn out in the service to his club, he has been a worthy ambassador for the club and well deserving of his MBE and Vice Presidency. He is a smashing bloke and always has a smile on his face.

So, for footballing excellence and outstanding loyalty, there can only be one candidate. For striking ability alone, I find it very close, but narrowly award my striker of all time to **STEVE BULL**, closely followed by **JIMMY MURRAY**, with John Richards in third place and Derek Dougan fourth. I can't give the award to Murray because he didn't score 300 goals and Bull did.

How lucky I am to have seen all four of them play for my club.

And just before I finish this chapter I must mention **Peter Knowles**. He was a player of supreme skill, impishness and arrogance and could have become almost as good as Peter Broadbent. Indeed, he could worthily have taken over Broadbent's role of ball playing scheming genius, one Peter following on from the other. He possessed most of Broadbent's skills (minus the body swerve) but substituted cheek and arrogance for the maestro's laid-back insouciance.

But PK played only five years for Wolves, sadly, before leaving to follow his conscience and his god. One wonders if he could possibly have seen his way to playing out his career before taking up his mission in life - to become a Jehovah's Witness. However, we should respect his very personal decision. What a talented player Wolves lost.

Chapter 26
The Good Times and the Bad

Sir Jack's good friend is Heyhoe-Flint.
But Rachael's cross that he's not skint
In paying for his boyhood sin
of dodging turnstiles to get in.

"Don't think you've paid your just deserts,
For Jack, you know, it really hurts
That some will boast to friends and say
'I watched the match but didn't pay'."

"It's types like you, Jack, give the game
a mostly undeserved bad name.
Why can't you just say: 'WHAT THE HECK!'
And write the club a decent cheque?"

"I'm not going to dwell on hard times in the rest of this book." This is what I said in the final paragraph of Chapter 7. And yet, here are some more bad times, but only included so that I can lead on to describe some much better ones which followed them.

The numbers three and fifteen have for long been etched on my brain. Why? It seems to be a reasonable question to ask. They can't be the score of a match. We would never win by 15 goals to three, and even Wolves wouldn't slump to an ignominious 3-15 defeat. So why would I have these numbers engrained in my consciousness for 52 years?

I am referring here to season 1964-65, the year Wolves' world fell apart and they were relegated. Wolves had been down through the divisions in their history before but surely a team who had reached the heights less than a decade previously had no business being in the 2nd Division? But it can happen to anyone, and it did happen to us.

The figures, 3 and 15, refer to the fact that we picked up just three points in the first fifteen matches of that season: one win, one draw and 13 defeats, with a goals record of 15 for and 42 against. An appalling start to a campaign, but at least we improved a little after that, with a record for the final 27 matches of:

W12 D3 L12 GF47 GA49 Pts 27

And so, we managed exactly a point a game for the matches after that utterly disastrous start, which might have been just enough to keep us up if averaged out over the whole season. But the damage had been done and Wolves were relegated.

Stan Cullis was sacked in September, but the new caretaker manager, Andy Beattie, didn't get off to a flyer himself, since Wolves lost all their matches in October. He did steady the ship a little bit after that but what the team needed was championship form to make up for the terrible start - what they got, in fact, was a mediocre to average performance. Perhaps no team has ever come back from gaining just 10 per cent of their available points from so many matches at the start of the season.

Beattie was kept on for the start of the 2nd Division campaign of 1965-66, but he didn't cover himself in glory, gaining four wins and suffering four defeats in the first eight matches. After the 9th match he was sacked, having lost that 9th match, perhaps appropriately, by 3 goals to 9! Yes, Southampton thumped us comprehensively on the south coast by a massive 9-3, an utter humiliation in a division in which we were expected to be one of the contenders for promotion. How could we recover from a second bad start - five defeats from nine matches and a goals record spoiled, in just one match, from 22-14 to 25-23?

We did it by appointing Ronnie Allen as manager and by wiping out the nine goals with four successive 3-0 wins. In fact, we were unbeaten in Allen's first 10 matches, ending with that famous 8-2 victory against Portsmouth, so we had achieved our south coast revenge. When Southampton came to Molineux later in the season we were unable to beat them, but stemmed the tide with a 1-1 draw.

Peter Knowles showed his class and ability through all the ups and downs of that turbulent start by scoring an amazing total of 14 goals in the first 16 matches, including one in the 3-9 debacle. Peter was such an obvious replacement for Broadbent, who was no longer with us, and we can only surmise as to what might have happened if he had carried on playing football.

Ronnie Allen was unable to salvage the mediocre start to the season, but the following season he took us back to our rightful place amongst the elite. This was after a titanic battle with Coventry City, who pipped us for the title and became established amongst the giants for many years. We, on the other hand, oscillated between the top leagues before plunging through the trapdoor and ending up in the bottom division.

Today, how different our respective circumstances are. We are (we hope) once again knocking on the door of the Premier League, whilst poor Coventry, proud members at the top level and sometime holders of the FA Cup, are now where we once were and in the bottom tier of league football. We wish them every success in the long climb back towards the upper echelons.

It is said that no team has a right to play in any division, and that is undoubtedly true. But it felt in those days that we, the great Wolves, should be nowhere else but at the top table with the other great sides. It took many years to accept the fact we had no such right and could even go out of the league completely, as we very nearly did. Accrington Stanley, one of the founder members of the football league, folded and had to be reincarnated later, and Preston North End, the old Invincibles who won the double in the first season of the league, have struggled in the lower divisions for the past many years. A team must earn the right to play in the top division and not expect it to be provided as a divine right.

The problem is again the un-level playing field, where the right to be at the top table is bought with hard cash and retained in the same way. Do we want Wolves to be a top team just because they can now throw lashings of cash at the problem? I sometimes wonder. As I watch yet another new manager taking over for the 2017-2018 season and witness the shipping in and out of many players I sometimes wonder: "Is this still my club and my team?" I think it is, because I will still follow them to the ends of the earth, come what may. They are Wolves, and so am I. It doesn't matter what owner or manager is in place or which players take to the pitch for us - that link cannot be broken. We are Wolves!

Is it possible to enjoy football in the lower leagues? It's certainly better winning every week rather than losing match after match. I and, I know for a fact, most of my Steve Bull buddies, thoroughly enjoyed the Kenny Jackett season in League One, when we seemed to win almost every time we turned out. Admittedly, we didn't want to be in that division but, finding ourselves in it, we made the very best of it, breaking club records galore and setting a new divisional record of 103 points. Our club records included a new best points' total (obviously 103), a record nine consecutive wins and five consecutive away wins, which equalled the start we made to the 1962-63 season. We were back in our now accustomed Championship division and ready to make another push for the top level. Who wouldn't have enjoyed that brief season in the third tier of English football?

Yet, to enjoy such a season at a lower level, one must either have never played at the highest level or have been demoted whilst there. I remember, when I was a commercial chemist, I played in a table tennis league for a team called the Alchemists. We were too good for the 2nd division but not good enough for the 1st. Consequently, we oscillated between the two, thoroughly enjoying winning in the 2nd but trudging along each week to inevitable defeat in the 1st. Although we were known as the Alchemists, the ancient chemists who claimed to be able to change lesser metals into gold, we never discovered the secret of transforming the silver of our 2nd level triumphs into the gold of 1st division mastery.

Mind you, we did find a source of gold at Wolves and that was from the generous wallet and even more generous heart of a gentleman named Jack (later Sir Jack) Hayward. Sir Jack was absolutely devoted, not to say besotted, with his beloved Wolves and he put his money where his mouth was, dipping his hand into his pocket and investing millions of pounds of his own fortune into the club that he loved. Perhaps it was his way of repaying the debt he owed to the club because of the entrance money he denied it when he crawled under the turnstiles as a very young lad! If so, he has repaid that debt many millions of times over.

I'm not going to expound in chapter and verse on all that Sir Jack has done for us. People much more qualified than me have done a far better job of it than I could ever do. Suffice it to say, he helped save the club from extinction, built a magnificent new stadium to replace the rotting corpse of the once noble stadium used in the glory days and provided funding to build a team fit to carry us to the top again. He was certainly a true supporter, ringing Rachael Heyhoe-Flint in the middle of the night from his home in the Bahamas to find out the score of the latest match (I know how he felt!). And who can forget the joy on his face as he gave the thumbs-up sign to many thousands of us golden-shirted devotees, packed into the Millennium Stadium on that momentous day in Cardiff?

Sir Jack has received much unjustified criticism. Why did he choose to live in the Bahamas for most of the year? Well, that's entirely his own business - and anyway, the tax he might have avoided was more than repaid by such gestures as buying the priceless Lundy Island in the Bristol Channel for the nation. Again, he has been pilloried for under-investing in the team when they gained their first promotion to the Premier League. That's a bit like responding to your grandmother's birthday gift of £100 by saying "Thanks very much, Nan, but you should have given me £200". Sir Jack's money was his, to do what he wanted with, and it seems that he very much wanted to plough a great deal of it into the coffers of Wolverhampton Wanderers.

I was privileged to be one of the fortunate supporters drawn by lottery to attend the great man's funeral in St Peter's Church, close to Molineux Stadium. A very moving and yet joyful service it turned out to be, culminating in a heartfelt and humorous address by his dear friend, Rachael Heyhoe-Flint. Sadly, we have now said our goodbyes to her as well, two giant and lifelong stalwarts of the Wolves, now happily reunited. Perhaps they both have twinkles in their eyes, wondering how we will all react to what they know is about to happen in the Wolves' long and proud history. Will it be more frustration and despair or are the great times about to resurrect themselves again? If we all keep our level of allegiance to Wolves on as high a plane as they did then the club will not be lacking in wonderful support,

I have spoken in this chapter of some dark and difficult times in our beloved team's history, but also of some happy and glorious occasions. I have one more very happy occasion, on a personal level, to recount and this will be the subject of the next chapter.

Chapter 27
What a Club Is Wolves!

Now, if I were a Leicester Fox,
Would they have given me a box?
And if I were a Derby Ram
I'd likely sit just where I am.

And if I were a West Brom Throstle
To reach my seat I'd trip and jostle.
And if I were a Brentford Bee
A box might be too good for me.

But no, I am an ardent Wolf;
From them to us there's quite a gulf.
If you're a Wolves fan you'll soon find
Our club can be so sweet and kind.

When it's too hard to reach the ground
They'll find some way to work around
the problem so that you can see
your final match in luxury.

For a good many years I have corresponded on football forums, email groups and message boards, to discuss all things Wolves. I can't remember what name we gave, if any, to our email forum back in the 90s and early years of the noughties but, my word, it could often make Molineux Mix seem like a vicarage tea party. It was run by something, or someone, called Majordomo, and Wolverhampton University housed the server that was its engine room.

There were two competing groups on the forum, the Happy Clappers and the Four Horsemen of the Apocalypse, with their acolytes, the doom mongers of impending Armageddon. I was mostly a Happy Clapper. We generally used our real names (which I won't reveal here), though some had pseudonyms like "The Grim Reaper" and JIWAL (John Ireland Whinge a lot). No prizes for guessing which side of the argument those two were on.

The Horsemen hated the Clappers with a vengeance, despising and ridiculing their optimism for Wolves' future, while we Happies despised their gloom and negativity and couldn't see how people with such pessimism could really be true Wolves supporters, as nothing about the club seemed to please them or cause them to be enthused. Some of it was probably a windup and, if so, I was well and truly taken in by it all.

I know the forum was still running in 2003 because I remember sending an inspirational (I hoped) email to all members of the list the night before Cardiff, urging them to support all we attendees with their thoughts and vibes, and to will us on to victory by the sheer force of their cosmic power. I was a bit of a dreamer and romantic back then (and think I probably still am)!

These days I am a member of the internet forum, Molineux Mix - or is it a message board, or even a blog? I joined it in 2009, so what happened in the six years from 2003 I can't recall. I think it is possible for one to be a sleeping member, so maybe I was one of those. In the period during which I have been an "active" member I have submitted two hundred posts, so I've not been very active at all - more a reader and a listener than a poster. Some of the postings from other "Mixers" seem very knowledgeable and erudite to my ears, while others are best forgotten. Some are very funny and others controversial. A bit of trolling sometimes occurs but is rapidly stamped on by the watchful Moderators. Generally, I don't feel qualified to join in the technical discussions. Although I have supported Wolves for nearly 60 years I am, like Sir Jack, unable to fathom some of the modern systems and jargon. He and I are from the era of centre-forwards and inside-lefts and know little about strikers or Number 10s!

I made one of my rare postings on 12th April, this year of 2017, the repercussions of which, to me, were enormous. I initiated a thread entitled "Swan Song", and, to paraphrase, this is what I said:

"I doubt I will get to Molineux again, with my Parkinson's now kicking in strongly, and that's a shame as 2nd November marks 60 years since I first attended. To mark my departure from Molineux, here's a short farewell in verse."

I then appended the poem which ends the Introduction to this book.

The result was almost instant, and totally dramatic. On the 12th there were 38 replies to the thread, by close of the day on 13th a further 18 replies came through and the thread received its 80th and last reply on 21st April. After the 53rd post I replied to my own thread to give Mixers some background to my history and condition.

In general, I feel it is bad form posting again on your own thread, laying one open to accusations of attention seeking as the thread is bumped up to the top of the pile and is the first to be seen by people logging on. Usually, a thread runs its course and then it is lost from the log-in screen, which is as it should be. Of course, it is sometimes necessary to reply to one's own thread if a question is asked or a refutation or clarification is needed.

Almost all responders were sympathetic to my plight, or in praise of the club and of certain Trojan workers on Molineux Mix, citing PumpKing and arctic rime especially. They, together with personnel from the club, had hatched a plot to lay on something very special for me on the last day of the 2016-17 season, when we would be playing Preston North End. In a coincidence of symmetry, Preston were our opponents in the last home match of my first season.

It still seems almost incomprehensible to me that, in their extraordinary generosity and warm heartedness, the club had seen fit to treat me, an ordinary and undeserving fan, to the use of a corporate box to watch the match, together with up to seven companions of my choice, completely free of charge. I was totally gobsmacked.

I was sent information and instructions by Marketing Manager, Laura Gabbidon, whom I met on the day and found to be a lovely lady. There are strict dress codes to be complied with - smart shoes and smart suits or dresses. Smart denims could be worn, but not faded or ripped ones. Shucks; that meant that my torn jeans wouldn't be acceptable! I went on a shopping spree with my wife to buy a smart outfit as my suits no longer fitted me. Bizarrely, one of the other banned items of apparel is club colours, including home colours. It's posh in them-there boxes!

The itinerary was posted to me; it was the last match of the season and all Championship fixtures kicked off at 12 noon.

1000 Arrive

1015 Food

1200 Kick off

1245 Half Time

1300 Second Half

1345 End of Match

1500 Bar Closes

But there would be more - much more!

I was delighted to invite, as my guests, Ann and Kevin, the faithful chauffeurs from my village, Jan and Ali (the mother and daughter) and their friend Wendy, all from Newport and all of them my Steve Bull Stand companions, and my brother, Joe and daughter, Rachel. I think they were all as much on Cloud Nine as I was.

The week before the great day was taken up with considerable nerves and tension as I willed my health to hold out and not let me down. I drool excessively and I prayed I wouldn't disgrace myself and dribble all over my new suit.

Sunday morning arrived and we were up at the crack of dawn. My wife helped me to dress in my finery and then, bang on time, Ann and Kevin arrived. We hardly recognised each other in our glad rags! We all piled into their car and were on our way to Molineux, our friends from Newport making their own way from Shropshire.

Parking was provided, conveniently right outside the Steve Bull Stand, and I didn't have far to walk into the very impressive executive suite. Down the carpeted corridor we padded and into the equally impressive Box Number 7 where we found Jan, Ali and Wendy already waiting for us. The window of the box looked out in a direct line with the goal line at the North Bank end. What a view it was, and an order of magnitude greater than the facilities offered to the standard spectator. But we were not standard spectators that day - we were royalty, and were being treated as such.

Before we had been there many minutes and had had a chance to take in our sumptuous surroundings, a team of most courteous and affable catering staff entered the box with platters of tasty-looking finger buffet items. That meant I wouldn't be struggling with knives and forks at a sit-down meal. Special dietary requirements were catered for and the staff could not have been more pleasant or obliging.

We were nearing the end of our repast when a very dapper and smartly-suited gentleman knocked on the door and entered the box. He didn't need to knock -

after all, it was his stand. The one and only Steve Bull, a genuine and special bloke, had taken the trouble to meet us for a photoshoot. It meant more than I can say and really made my day. I asked him if he was playing in the match; he replied that his knees had gone, and most other things as well. After his departure and as I sat and contemplated what was happening to me, tears welled in my eyes. This was to be my last day at Molineux and some very special people were making it very special indeed for me.

There was yet another surprise waiting for me. Another knock sounded at the door and another Wolves player entered the box. I was so confused and emotional after the Steve Bull visitation that I got this new player's identity confused:

"Danny! I'm delighted to see you. But shouldn't you be out on the pitch, warming up?" (I had seen Danny Batth's name on the team sheet).

"I'm not playing," said Matt Doherty, giving me a funny look. "My hamstring is better but they thought it best not to risk it." And then he presented me with the shirt he would have worn in the match, had his picture taken with me and then went off to find a marker pen so that he could sign the shirt for me.

The emotion generated by these wonderful gestures was almost too much, and I could feel the tears welling again.

Before the match started I had the great pleasure of briefly meeting PumpKing, one of the ringleaders involved in organising this great surprise. He is a charming man and his heart could not be more greatly committed to Wolves and the welfare of fellow supporters.

Then it was time for the match to start and we settled down in our seats. We weren't in them for long, as this wonderful club had organised one more special treat - a first minute goal for Wolves, right in front of our eyes, and magnificently headed home by Danny Batth from Jordan Graham's excellent corner. There were to be no more goals, but we thoroughly enjoyed the to-and-fro of the rest of the match, watching it all like Lords and Ladies.

In a box to our left we could see former club captain Jody Craddock. At half-time he left his box and appeared on the pitch to present a cheque to a disabled young boy, who was watching the match from the box to our right. We do wish every health and happiness to this young boy and to Jody's son.

The match over, our further needs were attended to and we were offered more drinks and availed ourselves of the palatial toilet facilities. The ladies were so enthralled by theirs that I suggested they took photos of them, to compare with the bog-standard facilities in the main concourse.

I briefly met Laura Gabbidon, a lovely lady, who had been instrumental in arranging this fabulous treat for unworthy me. The staff came in to clear away, still with lovely attitudes and smiles on their faces. They deserve top pay for what they do so well.

We were under no pressure whatsoever to vacate our box but, at length, we reluctantly left it, thanking everybody who had looked after us so well, as we returned to our cars. It was such an amazing send off to the end of a Molineux career and I cannot express my gratitude enough to those who had anything to do with arranging it. It demonstrates the caring and loving nature of the club and shows how it puts the fans' needs first. It also demonstrates the brotherhood and sisterhood of the Wolves supporters, and especially the Molineux Mixers, all united in a common bond - the bond of love for this great club of ours.

Talking of the members of the Molineux Mix forum, I forgot to mention, when describing the thread that I posted, which led to these stupendous happenings, the incredible offers of help received from very special people. Many people, who had no idea where I lived, nevertheless offered to run me to the ground to ease my match attendance difficulties, others offered to help in any way they could and one great guy, TrueWolf, on hearing that I intended to write this book, offered his professional expertise in designing the book's cover. And I also discovered that many of the respondents had, themselves, completed 60 years of service to this great club, some of them many more years than my record of 60. What had I done to deserve recognition and honour from the club, more than they? However unworthy I may be, I am greatly humbled and I love you all.

One last event put the final icing on the cake. I had sent a letter round via an intermediary - Adam from

Newport - to my pals in the J8 section of the Steve Bull Stand, saying goodbye, wishing them well and saying how much I had enjoyed their company over the years that I had sat with them. Accompanying the letter were some rather nice, top-of-the-market chocolates. The letter came back, annotated with lovely and moving comments but it was unaccompanied by any chocolates which might have been left over as surplus to requirements! Obviously, all the chocolates provided were required and there were none to spare at the end.

Chapter 28
I Hate...

We put up with Nottingham Forest,
We put up with Liverpool too.
We put up with West Bromwich Albion,
But Wanderers we love you.

We put up with Coventry City,
We put up with Leicester too.
We put up with West Ham United,
But P [...] I HATE you.

What an unpleasant title for what was intended to be the last chapter of this book, particularly after the joy of the previous chapter. I shall have to write a further chapter or two with more friendly titles and themes. What or whom do I hate, then, if not the clubs cited in the verse above?

Surprisingly, I don't hate Leeds United, even though they deprived us of a Cup Final place in 1973.

I don't hate Liverpool, even though they bought Alun Evans from us and then beat us 6-0 at our place the following week.

I don't hate Manchester United, even though they advanced from being close rivals of ours in the 50s to become the most successful team ever known, while we declined, to become relative nonentities - well, I don't hate them very much!

I don't hate Chelsea.
I don't hate Arsenal.
I don't hate Manchester City.
I don't hate Birmingham City.
I don't hate Sunderland.
I don't hate Aston Villa.
I don't hate Nottingham Forest.
I don't hate West Bromwich Albion!!!
I don't even hate Bolton Wanderers!!!!!!!!!!!!!!!!

For God's sake, then, whom or what is it that I hate?

I'm not a hating sort of person. Rather, I try to love people, or at least tolerate them. But what I do hate with a vengeance is the cursed PARKINSON'S DISEASE, PD, MR P. I hate him from the depths of my being, I loathe him from the pit of my soul, I hate, detest, revile and abominate him. GET OUT OF MY LIFE MR P. I want no truck with you.

I took good care of my body during my working life and hoped for a good retirement. I've been an active athlete most of my life and was greatly looking forward to retirement, when I would have had all the time in the world to race and train. During the working-week it had been necessary to run in the evenings and, in the wintertime, that meant gritting one's teeth, muffling up and venturing out into the freezing darkness. There was no other way, if success was to be attained. But, come retirement, I hoped to be able to train any time of the day and, even in winter, to get out in the daylight and run over the countryside, rather than be forced onto the roads or running boring laps round a floodlit track. What a pleasant prospect to look forward to!

But before this could be realised and enjoyed, Mr P. had me in his clutches and put paid to all that, and

I HATE HIM FOR IT.

He didn't take me bravely and boldly but, like the coward that he is, crept up insidiously on me, working his evil spells on my brain and body for 10 years, before being outed by the neurologist.

I HATE HIM FOR THAT.

PD is thought to be non-genetic but, although my dear mother suffered so badly with his malign presence, he still came after me, against all statistical odds.

I HATE HIM FOR THAT.

I worked in a chemical laboratory for some years, and some of the chemicals I had to deal with can induce PD in certain people. Mr P. decided I would be one of those people and

I HATE HIM FOR IT.

I started slowly with PD and was not too badly affected, although my walking was ungainly and my speech started to lose its resonance and clarity. I began to drool embarrassingly and started to fumble with fine motor movements, like tying laces, doing up buttons and getting coins out of my purse. And so

I HATE HIM FOR ALL OF THAT.

The PD medication gave me water retention, swollen legs and disturbed or sleepless nights.

I HATE HIM FOR THAT.

Sometimes I would have vivid dreams and physically act them out, before taking medication to stop this potentially dangerous behaviour. Thus, one night, in a dream, I was playing in goal and, to the consternation of my wife, I dived out of bed to tip the ball round the post, taking most of the duvet with me. I remembered every detail of the dream afterwards. As we both found the incident both disturbing and amusing.

I mildly HATE HIM FOR THAT.

I have slowly become more bent over, slow and weak and

I HATE HIM FOR THAT.

Sometimes I am so weak I can hardly lift my foot up to put it in my shoe or trouser leg and

I HATE HIM FOR THAT.

I have become deeply depressed and have been put on antidepressants, for which

I HATE HIM.

In company, people can't hear what I say and so they turn away and ignore me. When things are quiet, I might try to contribute to the conversation, but either my words will come out slurred or they will be too soft, so I will be considered a doddery old fool and dismissed contemptuously, and for that

I REALLY HATE HIM WITH A VENGEANCE.

And, above all, he has made me too incapacitated to attend my beloved Molineux anymore and

I HATE, LOATHE, DESPISE AND DETEST HIM FOR THAT.

Writing this book has made me aware of several things that I wasn't fully aware of before I started writing it, such as how short Wolves reign of glory had really been and what a loving fellowship is the family of Wolves supporters. But what I was totally unaware of was the all-consuming anger and rage that burned within me for all things PD. I thought I was very accepting of my condition, philosophical about it and realising that I had been unlucky enough to draw the short straw. But that was all a façade; I wasn't really accepting it at all and the anger has remained suppressed and unrecognised up to now.

Let's leave it until tomorrow and see how my hatred is then.

Well tomorrow has come and I find that writing this chapter has been a very cathartic exercise for me. I have been able to recognise the anger and I think it has now gone, or at least abated. I no longer hate MR P. with all my being. It's not his fault, poor chap. He's just an evil spirit, put on this earth to find his ten million annual victims, and maybe he was below his totals when he came for me, not a nice position in which to find himself, in these days of targets and quotas. I'll give him the benefit of the doubt and bear my Parkinson's with as much courage and cheerfulness as my very dear mother bore hers.

Particularly, I'll try to banish the feelings of self-pity which were welling up in the first part of this chapter. If you can't change something, then you need to accept it, and I'll continue to fight him whenever and wherever it is possible to do so.

I hope that I am now at last REALLY accepting of my condition and I will make the best of things and, who knows, a cure may soon be found. I think the antidepressant is kicking in already! What you can't change, don't worry about, but, where there's hope, pursue all avenues vigorously, and realise that many, many people are far worse off than yourself. It's good to be alive. And I will continue to follow my dear Mum's example and bear my Parkinson's as valiantly as she did.

On this happier and more positive note I'll end the chapter with the ditty we used to sing in years gone by:

> *We hate Nottingham Forest,*
> *We hate Liverpool too.*
> *We hate West Bromwich Albion,*
> *But Wanderers we love you.*

Chapter 29
There's Only One Wanderers

A number of clubs have the label "City",
which, since it's so common, is quite a pity.
But moving from them to a lot nearer home,
Our tag denotes players who just love to roam.

In just a few moments a quiz will appear,
So, I'd best bring an end to this stanza right here;
For, if I have anything much more to say,
I'll probably give all the answers away.

We often like to chant the mantra:

There's Only One Wanderers

And it is true: there is only one Wolverhampton Wanderers, but we are not alone in attaching this tag to our name. There are two other Wanderers in the football league, Bolton and Wycombe, and so we don't have exclusive use of this tag. In fact, we were not even the first to make use of it. The team we love to hate, dear old Bolton, adopted the appellation in 1877, while we didn't do so until 1879, so we can't claim first usage. Sadly, we are not the unique Wanderers of the football league, nor are we even the first. We even share the initials WWFC with Wycombe, so we are quite ordinary in descriptive terms.

Some teams have shown enough originality to be the only one's bearing a unique tag. For example, Crewe is the only "Alexandra" in the whole league.

In contrast, a large proportion of teams are unimaginative enough to append no tag at all to their name. Chelsea would be an example of such an uncreative side.

There are three tags which are used by a total of 38 clubs.

Just to see what your knowledge of the league is like, try answering these quiz questions without looking at the answers, which will be shown on a separate page. All answers apply to the football league as at the start of the 2017-18 season.

QUESTIONS

1. How many teams have no tag appended to their name? (1 point if you get within plus or minus 2 of the actual answer);

2. Name these teams (1 point for each correct answer; minus 1 point for each incorrect answer);

3. What are the three most common tags and name the teams associated with each? (1 point for each correct answer; minus 1 point for each incorrect answer).

4. Which tags have 3 teams associated with them, other than "Wanderers"?

5. Name the tags and teams associated with question 4 (again 1 point for each correct answer and minus 1 point for each incorrect answer);

6. Which tag is associated with just 2 teams? (Hint: this tag comes before the club's name, rather than after it). Name the teams;

7. How many teams have a unique tag, for example, Crewe (Alexandra)? (1 point if you get within plus or minus 1 of the actual answer);

8. Name these teams (1 point for each correct answer; minus 1 point for each incorrect answer).

9. Which team has the most letters in its name plus tag, including spaces? For example: "Crewe Alexandra" has 15 letters.

10. Which team has the second most letters, including tag and spaces?

11. The nickname for our team is "WOLVES", containing 6 letters. Name the team(s) which have fewer letters in their nickname.

12. Which tag has 4 teams associated with it? Name those teams.

When you have answered the questions turn to the next page for the answers.

ANSWERS

1. Twenty-six teams have no tag;

2. They are:

    Arsenal; Barnsley; Barnet; Blackpool; Brentford; Burnley; Bury; Chelsea;
    Chesterfield; Crystal Palace; Everton; Fulham; Gillingham; Liverpool;
    Middlesbrough; Millwall; Morecambe; Portsmouth; Port Vale; Reading;
    Rochdale; Southampton; Stevenage; Sunderland; Walsall; Watford;

3. The three most common tags are City, Town and United;

    CITY: Birmingham; Bradford; Bristol; Cardiff; Coventry; Exeter; Hull;
    Leicester; Lincoln; Manchester; Norwich; Stoke; Swansea;
    TOWN: Cheltenham; Crawley; Fleetwood; Grimsby; Huddersfield; Ipswich;
    Luton; Mansfield; Northampton; Shrewsbury; Swindon; Yeovil;
    UNITED: Cambridge; Carlisle; Colchester; Leeds; Manchester; Newcastle;
    Oxford; Peterborough; Rotherham; Scunthorpe; Sheffield;
    Southend; West Ham;

4. The tags with 3 teams associated with them (other than Wanderers) are:

   ALBION, ATHLETIC and COUNTY

5. ALBION: Brighton & Hove, Burton and West Bromwich;

   ATHLETIC: Charlton, Oldham and Wigan;
   COUNTY: Derby, Newport and Notts.

6. The tag is AFC: Bournemouth and Wimbledon.

7. 10 teams have a unique tag.

8. They are:

   Alexandra (Crewe), Argyle (Plymouth), Dons (Milton Keynes),
   Forest (Nottingham), Hotspur (Tottenham), North End (Preston),
   Rangers (Queens Park), Stanley (Accrington); Villa (Aston) and
   Wednesday (Sheffield).

9. Wolverhampton Wanderers (23)

10. Brighton & Hove Albion (22)

11. "Man U" (5) and "Spurs" (5).

12. The tag is "Rovers": Blackburn, Bristol, Doncaster and Forest Green.

That's a total of 112 points going begging. Multiply your total by 0.9 to get your percentage score.

I hope you did well. At least our club won one award - most letters in its name!

Chapter 30
Tying up Loose Ends

Tom Phillipson, in days of yore,
knew just exactly how to score.
He was a simply magic player,
And then became the town's Lord Mayor.

You'll never find a wing half slicker
than Kenneth Hunt, a local vicar.
He'd go down on his knees and pray,
then run onto the pitch and play.

Another striker, Jesse Pye,
was very pleasing on the eye.
His games/goals ratio - 2.2,
Was very close to you know who!

Now, if you seek an honest man,
Then Cullis is the man - our Stan;
And, as for players, who's the best?
P Broadbent betters all the rest.

It used to annoy me in my days as an athlete when a certain member of our athletics club would come up with a whole catalogue of reasons why he had just failed to beat his personal best time over a certain distance.

"If I hadn't had to work so late and taken a late tea I would have knocked a couple of seconds off, and then the wind was troublesome in the back straight - worth another second at least. So, there we have it - I should be the club record holder over 3,000 metres, and not you."

Yes, but you're not, Mike. I've done the time and you haven't, and I'm the record holder and you're not. If you want the record, go out and get it, but don't make excuses if you fail.

The reason I bring this up is because we can compare players, who might have been the best if circumstances had been different, with other players who are considered the best because of what they have, in fact, actually achieved. So, we all know that Steve Bull is the greatest goal scorer who ever donned a Wolves shirt, hitting the net 306 times in 561 matches, but what about a certain player from another era who scored 170 goals in 234 appearances? If he had played 561 games, like Bull, and continued to score at his same average rate he would have ended his career with 408 goals to his credit. But he didn't, and Bull is the highest goal scorer by a mile. I'll tell you who this player from the past is later.

There is obviously a generational aspect in the qualities that fans consider when rating their favourite players. Obviously, a 15-year-old lad today can't rate Steve Bull at first hand, because Bull retired before he was born. He can only hear about his brilliance from those who have seen him, or he can read about him in books, or watch him on videos. But it would be wrong of him to dismiss Bull because he is from before his time, and it would also be wrong for him to declare "I think Nouha Dicko is the best striker Wolves have ever had" without, at least, considering the evidence from the past.

Similarly, people reading this book might say "Why does he keep banging on about Broadbent and Deeley and Wright? They're ancient history and irrelevant to us." That would be sad and misguided - such players as they shaped Wolves' history and provided happy memories to me and others. But I, in turn, must be careful not to dismiss the players before my time, but actively seek out information, mostly from books now, as witnesses are fast dying out, or have already shuffled off this mortal coil.

In this book, I have been telling you about players you may have mostly never seen. In the rest of this part of the chapter I will talk about a selection of players who played even before my time.

So back to that mystery striker who scored 408 (or, more accurately, 408-170=238) virtual goals for Wolves. His name was Billy Hartill and he was a prolific scorer for us in the years 1929 to 1935. I would have loved to have watched him ply his trade.

An even more exciting, though very slightly less prolific, goal scorer was Tom Phillipson, who scored 111 goals in only 159 games, a games-per-goals ratio of 1.432, which would have given him 391 goals from Bully's 561 games. His most exciting period came in the 1929-30 season when, in a period of 13 consecutive matches, he scored no fewer than 22 goals, including one hat-trick and one nap hand (five goals). I think he might well be, although I don't know for certain, the only Wolves player ever to score in 13 successive matches. He wasn't bad as a junior player either; in one match in which his side triumphed by scoring 15 goals, Tom's personal contribution was 14! He must have been feeling tired in the next match, since he managed to hit the net only 10 times.

When Tom retired he was active in local council work and became Lord Mayor of Wolverhampton.

The only ordained minister of religion to play for Wolves, as far as I can ascertain, was the Reverend Kenneth Hunt. He was a dynamic wing half in the style of Ron Flowers and his great claim to fame was that he scored one of the three goals by which Wolves beat the favourites Newcastle United 3-1 in 1908 to win the FA Cup for the second time. This was a shock win for Wolves as they were then in the 2nd Division.

Oh, to have seen the truly great Wolves team who won the Cup for the third time in 1949! They beat Leicester City 3-1 and the team was

Williams; Pritchard; Springthorpe; Crook; Shorthouse; Wright; Hancocks; Smyth; Pye; Dunn; Mullen.

Reports tell us that Sammy Smyth, the Irishman, scored one of the best goals ever seen in a Wembley final, with Jesse Pye getting the other two: Pye was another great striker for Wolves, scoring 95 goals in 209 matches.

This match saw the first of many club honours for the great Billy Wright, playing at wing half at that time, before he became established at centre half some years later, in season 1954-55.

The centre half in that Wembley win was Bill Shorthouse, who gave Wolves fabulous service between the years 1947 and 1957, playing in 376 matches. He was so consistent and dependable that he was never dropped from the team, neither by Ted Vizard, the manager in his first season, nor by Stan Cullis thereafter.

Those great wingers, Johnny Hancocks and Jimmy Mullen supplied the ammunition from the flanks in that 1949 Final. I've already talked about Mullen, whom I was lucky enough to see play, but unfortunately missed Hancocks, the tiny winger with the dynamic shot. He had a great scoring record for a winger, totalling 168 goals in 378 matches, probably one of the best, if not THE best, games per goal ratio of any Wolves winger.

In goal was the peerless Bert Williams, a lovely man, whose agility earned him the name of "The Cat". It is a great regret of mine that I missed seeing Bert play by one season. I once saw him interviewed on TV, by the late, great Brian Moore, I think it was. Bert came across as the perfect gentleman and told his favourite joke:

A man went into a local store in Glasgow to buy an item and, as he walked out, the proprietor, a Scotsman, noticed the customer had left his change on the counter. The absent-minded customer happened to glance through the window, as he walked away from the shop, and was surprised to see the proprietor tapping gently on the glass with a sponge to remind him (not very forcefully) of his forgotten change.

This was a mischievous dig at what Bert considered to be the parsimony of the Scots.

I was lucky enough to meet Bert a day or two after that programme. I was purchasing a ticket in the Wolves ticket office when I heard a familiar voice at the service point next to me:

"I believe you have a ticket for me to collect." I turned:

"Mr Williams?" and shook the great man's hand.

Just as the 1949 Cup Final was the first of Billy Wright's individual title wins, so it was manager Stan Cullis's first of many managerial successes. Despite missing out on title wins as a player, he more than made up for it as manager, with two FA Cups and three League Championships as his proud legacy. He served Wolves for 30 years as player, assistant manager and manager and was a supremely determined and uncompromising centre half, brilliant in the air and, above all, scrupulously honest and fair. In the final match of the 1946-47 season Wolves were playing Liverpool at Molineux and needed to avoid defeat to lift their first ever Championship title. A Liverpool player broke through on goal when the score was 1-0 to Liverpool and Stan had the option of bringing him down to keep the scores within bounds. But, a man of integrity, he did not commit a foul, Liverpool scored a second and Wolves lost the match 1-2 and failed to win the title. You can't imagine such an action in today's cynical age. "One for the team" is the mantra, as the defender commits a professional foul and is (possibly) sent off.

And so, I end my commentary on Wolves players of long ago, fittingly with Stan Cullis, a man who epitomises all that is good about Wolves. He was the main architect of the glory days and, without him, those days would not have occurred. What big shoes they are that any future Wolves manager must fill!

There is one more thing to consider—who is the greatest ever Wolves player, whether seen by me or not? It's very difficult for me to compare players I have seen with those I haven't, and equally hard to compare defenders with strikers and goalies with playmakers. But I think you'll know, if you've been concentrating, who, from many wonderful contenders, I hold as my all-time greatest player. And that man is

PETER BROADBENT

I wouldn't be surprised at all if everybody, when asked to name their greatest-ever player, would always choose a player from their own era, one they have seen for themselves. I have done that and I bet you would do the same.

Chapter 31
Au Revoir, Not Goodbye

It's animals, runs, Wolves and love
that fall in showers from above.

And PD won't give me the hump;
I'll tell him: "Take a running jump!"

"You've got a very jaundiced view
But I'll still visit Molineux."

If I can't get there literally
I'll still be present virtually.

And so, I have come sadly to the end of my book. I've thoroughly enjoyed writing it, and I hope you have gained pleasure too in reading it. Many incidents have been forgotten, many players unmentioned, many joys and sorrows lost in the mists of time. But, throughout the book, I've tried to interweave the five main themes, which are:

1. Love
2. Athletics
3. Animals
4. Parkinson's
5. WOLVES.

These have been the five factors around which my life has revolved and I will summarise each of them in turn.

LOVE:

The book has described my love for my family and our pets, for my all-absorbing athletics hobby and to my all-encompassing devotion to my football team, Wolves. You'll notice that the only one of the five threads about which Love has nothing to say is Parkinson's, although one can say that the devotion, care and help shown by family and friends to deal with the condition is truly humbling and is the essence of love. So, in that sense, Parkinson's gives rise to love from caring friends and family.

ATHLETICS:

I use the term 'Athletics' to include the disciplines of track, road and cross country running, though strictly speaking it should also include field events, such as throwing and jumping, but these I didn't take part in, being thin and puny!

From early days I loved running, being not very good at ball games, and I devoted 40 years of my life to it, averaging over 1500 miles of running a year. You may have been irritated by the chapters devoted to this subject, but it has been an integral part of my life, and the chapters devoted to this subject illustrate the struggles of conscience I grappled with on many occasions; they have described how, on some occasions, I missed a football match so that I could run instead while, on other occasions, my obsession with Wolves caused me to bunk off running. And therefore, I suppose that I was just about equally committed to both running and to Wolves.

ANIMALS:

I have described an absolute menagerie of pets we gave refuge to, at one time or another and have shown how one single pet can be a soulmate and a devoted friend. I refer, of course, to my beloved and long-lamented dog, Kim.

PARKINSON'S

I hope I have explained what PD is and what it has done to me. I don't intend to rail any more against it here, but simply to state that it has been successful in ending my Molineux career - unless something turns up to beat it, of course!

WOLVES:

They are the love of my life, after my family of course. I hope this book has demonstrated my devotion to Wolves and what they mean to me. I wait, like you, for our Chinese owners - and, if not them, then somebody else - to raise us to the lofty heights again, from whence we can look down, not to gloat but to say "We are back in our rightful place at last. We are top dogs and we mean to remain so. We can proudly say; "Wolves for ever, ay we!"

Parkinson's has put an end to my Molineux visits, but it will not and cannot end my support for the team.

And now, to summarise my favourite (or un-favourite!) choices from the many described in this book:

Best player over all: Peter Broadbent;

Best goalie: Malcolm Finlayson and Bert Williams equally;
Best full back: Derek Parkin and Bobby Thomson equally;
Best wing half: Ron Flowers; Mike Bailey and Rev Kenneth Hunt equally;
Best centre half: Billy Wright and Bill Slater equally;
Best left winger: David Wagstaffe;
Best right winger: Kenny Hibbitt;
Best striker: Steve Bull;
Best goal poacher Norman Deeley;
Most charismatic player: Derek Dougan;

Best pet: Kim;
Best team: WOLVES;
Funniest incident: Den Haag's three own goals;
Most bizarre match: Everton in the fog, when the pitch was barely visible;
Most enjoyable match: Wembley (1974) and Cardiff (2003) equally;
Best stadium attended: Molineux Stadium;
Biggest disappointment: Missing out on the Cup / League double and a treble of successive Championship titles by a single point margin in 1960;

Best internet forum: Molineux Mix;
Most annoying sound: The Pompey bell;
Most pleasing sound: The crowd's reaction to a Wolves goal.

That just about wraps it up. Let's hope these stories of Wolves from long ago will be pleasing to Wolves fans and make the rest of the football community recognise the great team that we once were and are striving to become again. They will know we aren't just a tin-pot organisation but a famous football club with rich traditions, culture and history. We have had our dark days but have come through them and now look forward to the bright hope of a golden future.

Some devastating news broke, just before I sent this book to the printers - Carl Ikeme, our regular goalie and the gentle giant, was found to be suffering from leukaemia. This awful news leaves us all numbed but we know that great strides have been made in the treatment of this and many other diseases. We trust and pray that Carl will come through this battle a winner, and we'll keep a place warm for him between the Molineux goalposts. Good luck, Carl, in the biggest battle of your life. The whole Wolves community, and others throughout football, are right behind you and will be with you every inch of the way in your tough journey to recovery.

In chapter five I mentioned that one of our Kilimanjaro climbs was in aid of helping leukaemia sufferers. If our efforts prove to have helped Carl in any way then those efforts will have been doubly worthwhile.

Goodbye, readers, and fellow Wolves fans. I love you all. But, before I go, see the next page for a farewell poem, expressing my regrets at having to leave you, but holding out great hope for the future.

The tear drops in my eyes have started welling -
To Molineux I can't go any more.
I won't hear all the chanting and the yelling
I'll have to stay at home and close the door.
I'll get the crucial updates from Jeff Stelling,
Who'll keep me posted on the latest score.
Jeff's full of repartee and jibes and jest,
But watching on the box is second best.

I really want to see them at the ground;
To not be able to is just unfair.
I like to have my buddies all around
And sit among familiar faces there.
Whenever Wolves score there's a thunderous sound,
And, if it's ruled offside, we'll curse and swear.
The TV screen at home is not a patch
on really being present at the match.

But I'm not going to rant, complain or whine;
I'm fortunate to follow them at all.
Wherever watching, just to see them climb
And hope that they don't subsequently fall
But win promotion - that will be just fine
And lead to joy unbounded for us all.
Next year they'll win most home games that they play
And be invincible when they're away.

EPILOGUE

JAN: "Hello, Chris! What a surprise to meet you here! I thought you couldn't see any point in watching football."

CHRIS: "You're right, Jan, I can't, but when Laura offered Lawrence another box for what he tells me is the match to end all matches I felt I had to come along with him and make sure he's safe. He gets rather impulsive with this new medication he's on and is liable to run onto the pitch, or something."

LAWRENCE: "I can hear every word you're saying about me. I'm going to sit here in this box and soak up the atmosphere and enjoy this amazing occasion. How kind it is of Laura to offer me this super-posh box again - and she's even allowed me to wear my club colours this time! I feel a fraud now for celebrating my last match at Molineux a year ago - and here I am, doing it again, in 2018."

CHRIS: "What's so special about tonight, then? Isn't it just another football match?"

LAWRENCE: "You think it's just 'ANOTHER FOOTBALL MATCH'? It's the Championship play-off final, here at Molineux, between us - the mighty WOLVES - and Blackburn Rovers - two famous old clubs who've both won major honours in the past. One of them will make it back to the top again tonight and let it be us, oh please, do let it be us!!! And no shouting for Blackburn, Ann, or you're out of this box!"

ANN: "I like them to win for my Dad's sake, but not tonight - CERTAINLY NOT TONIGHT!"

LAWRENCE: "I've just realised; we can't be playing Blackburn. They were relegated to League One at the end of last season. What the heck - it doesn't matter who we're playing, just so long as we win!"

CHRIS: "I thought finals were played at Wembley, or some other important stadium?"

LAWRENCE: "Wash your mouth out, traitorous wife! Molineux is the most important stadium in the world, home of the greatest team of the 1950s, and soon to become the home of the greatest team of the late 2010s and the 2020s and beyond. The reason we are here tonight is that the final at tin pot Wembley last week ended 0-0 after extra time and the penalty shoot-out hadn't been decided after 20 minutes. Consequently, the referee abandoned the match and said it would have to be replayed as soon as possible; hence this midweek fixture. We won the toss and it's being played here."

CHRIS: "Well, it's very agreeable at night. The floodlights lend a sort of magic to it."

LAWRENCE: "What happened to your view that it's madness to sit outside in a field on a cool evening, when you could watch it at home in the company of Jeff Stelling?"

CHRIS: "We're not in a field - we're in an executive box <I don't think he really understands football>."

JAN: "We'll ignore the domestic they're having over there, Ali, and watch the match. It's just about to kick off. What an atmosphere! You can feel it inside the box."

CHRIS: "Well, surprisingly enough, I've quite enjoyed the game. I must admit it was quite exciting, beyond my expectations. Who's won?"

ANN; "Nobody has. There's a few seconds of extra time to go and we're all nervous wrecks. My God - a through ball from Neves to Costa. He's tripped. It's a **PENALTY!!!!!!!**"

CHRIS: "Why are all the non-gold players surrounding the referee? He's caught in the centre of a circle of hostile players, all pushing and shoving and arguing. What's going on?"

ANN: "They can argue until the cows come home (rather an apt remark at the old Cow Shed end) but it's a stonewall penalty. The ref won't change his mind. Oh, there's a knock at the door - could you see who it is please Kevin."

BULLY: "Good evening Lawrence. Come with me quickly."

LAWRENCE: "It's Bully again! He always visits me in my box. Matt Doherty should be along soon."

CHRIS: "I'll come too, to make sure he's safe."

JAN: "It's all right Chris - Bully will look after him."

BULLY: "Follow me through this way. If we stand here, right behind the goal, you'll have a bostin view of the penalty kick that takes us back to the Premier League."

LAWRENCE: "Thanks, Bully."

CHRIS; "LOOK AT THAT. Lawrence is down by the pitch. What's he doing there? I'll go down and bring him back."

LAWRENCE: "<The ref has finally broken loose from the melee and placed the ball on the spot; now for it! When he turns around the other way I'll sprint on before Bully can stop me and take the kick myself. I've got my kit on and no one will notice. It's my destiny to repay the club their kindness by scoring the winning goal>."

KEVIN: "Is that Costa taking the kick, Ann? It doesn't look a lot like him."

ANN: "Oh my God - it's Lawrence!!! He'll miss and the ref will blow for time. God preserve us!"

LAWRENCE: "<Here we go. I'll take a short run up and hammer it in the top corner>"

ANN: "I can't bear to watch. Oh my God, he hits the angle of bar and post, the ball bounces off the goalie's back, onto Lawrence's head and over the top. If only he'd taken a longer run-up it wouldn't have bounced off his head and he could have hammered it back in. Now we're doomed to a penalty shoot-out, which we're sure to lose."

CHRIS: "Well I'm glad to see Bully's looking after him. That was a thrilling match. Did you all enjoy it?"

LAWRENCE: "Oh Bully, I'm so sorry for that miss. Please let me take one of the shoot-out penalties and make amends. NO, PLEASE DON'T DRAG ME OFF THE PITCH!"

CHRIS: "Don't shout out in the night, love. Why are you so upset? You must have forgotten to take your pill and you've had a vivid dream again. Tell me about it."

LAWRENCE: "Oh sweetheart, thank God! I didn't lose the match for us after all. It was just one of PD's silly dreams - I'm so relieved. And now that this wonder drug is undergoing clinical trials I may yet find myself in my seat again next season, roaring them on to promotion. In fact, season 2017-18 hasn't finished yet and we're right up there and hot tips for promotion this season. Wolves are going up!"

"It shows how much I love my team - the fact that I could have such a passionate dream about them."

CHRIS: "I'm happy for you, dear. Goodnight and sweet drea... er, here's your tablet. Sleep well."

LAWRENCE: "Yes, hope springs eternal. We WILL become the top team in the world again, and very soon, and I WILL defeat Parkinson's. And I WILL teach you to understand football eventually, I hope (although the bookies would lay long odds against that!) Good night darling; see you in the Champions League!"

Printed in Great Britain
by Amazon